Village Walks
in
DERBYSHIRE

C000088313

Village Walks
in
DERBYSHIRE

Charles Wildgoose

COUNTRYSIDE BOOKS
NEWBURY, BERKSHIRE

First published 1997
© Charles Wildgoose 1997

All rights reserved.
No reproduction permitted without the prior
permission of the publisher:

COUNTRYSIDE BOOKS
3 Catherine Road
Newbury, Berkshire

ISBN 1 85306 461 0

Designed by Graham Whiteman
Photographs and maps by the author

Produced through MRM Associates Ltd., Reading
Printed by Woolnough Bookbinding Ltd., Irthlingborough

Contents

INTRODUCTION   8

WALK

1   ROWARTH ($4\frac{1}{2}$ miles)   10

2   EDALE ($6\frac{1}{4}$ miles)   14

3   BRADWELL ($3\frac{3}{4}$ miles)   18

4   TIDESWELL ($6\frac{3}{4}$ miles)   23

5   SHELDON (6 or 5 miles)   28

6   PILSLEY (6 miles)   33

7   BARLOW ($4\frac{1}{2}$ miles)   37

8   BARLBOROUGH ($7\frac{1}{4}$ miles)   41

9   ROWSLEY ($4\frac{1}{2}$ miles)   46

10   HOLYMOORSIDE ($5\frac{3}{4}$ miles)   51

11   TISSINGTON (4 miles)   55

12   HOGNASTON ($3\frac{3}{4}$ miles)   59

13   CROMFORD ($3\frac{3}{4}$ miles)   63

14   SOUTH WINGFIELD ($3\frac{1}{2}$ miles)   67

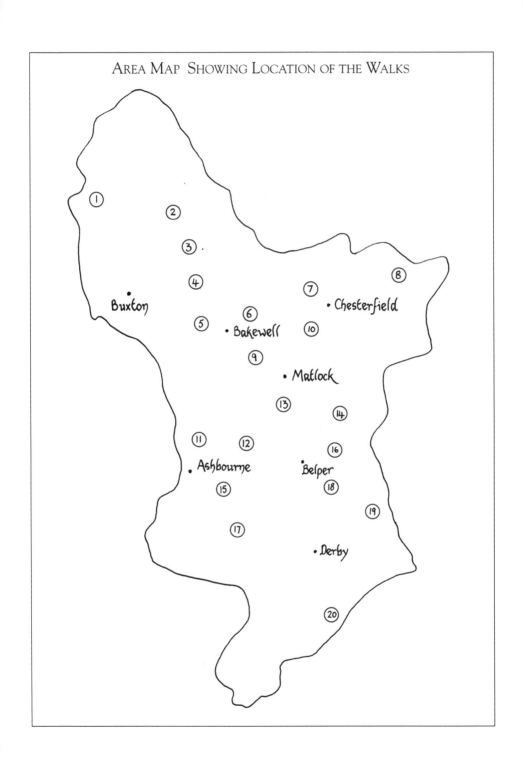

Area Map Showing Location of the Walks

WALK

15 OSMASTON (6¼ or 4½ miles)   72

16 HEAGE (4¼ miles)   76

17 LONGFORD (2 or 4½ miles)   80

18 HOLBROOK (6 miles)   84

19 WEST HALLAM (6 miles)   88

20 MELBOURNE (4¼ miles)   92

❧

Publisher's Note

We hope that you obtain considerable enjoyment from this book; great care has been taken in its preparation. Although at the time of publication all routes followed public rights of way or permitted paths, diversion orders can be made and permissions withdrawn.

We cannot of course be held responsible for such diversion orders and any inaccuracies in the text which result from these or any other changes to the routes nor any damage which might result from walkers trespassing on private property. We are anxious though that all details covering the walks are kept up to date and would therefore welcome information from readers which would be relevant to future editions.

Introduction

In this, my third book, I have included a number of villages and areas that many of you have probably not walked in before. Indeed they were new to me! Heage, Rowarth and Barlborough were just three of the villages I'd never visited before starting this book.

Only eight of the twenty walks are in the Peak District but this does not detract from the pleasure you will have in using this book. There is such a variety of villages in Derbyshire ranging from Rowarth with its lovely old millworkers' cottages in the far north to the much larger village of Melbourne in the south – Melbourne with the very impressive 11th and 12th-century St. Michael's church. There are other delights to discover outside the Peak District such as the wonderful thatched cottages of Osmaston, Heage Windmill, Wingfield Manor, Carsington Reservoir, the Great Pond of Stubbing – I could go on . . .

In addition to the walks there are suggestions as to what else you can do in the vicinity of each village – other places of interest. Some of these only open during the summer, some of them for part of the week only. Do check beforehand otherwise you may be disappointed.

All the walks have been checked by an ever growing band of willing volunteers namely Paul Hopkins, Peter Corke, Ian Swindell and Sandra Measures, Bob and Margaret Bacon, Paul and Ian Stanley, Jamie Wildgoose, Hannah Cooper, THE Phil Hawksworth, Dave Gregson, Katy Wildgoose and Justin Bonsall, Chris and Julia Gale, John Bradley, Muriel and Bryan Crapper and, of course, Balkees – I should like to thank them all for their help.

The walks can be followed using just the sketch maps and descriptions in the book. However, it is always as well to have the appropriate Ordnance Survey sheet with you. The countryside changes fairly rapidly albeit in only small ways sometimes. So if a wall or hedge is removed, a path diverted or a permissive path closed, you can find your way with the help of the OS map – and they are always useful too for identifying the main features of views. I have given the number and name of the relevant 1:25 000 scale map, Pathfinder or Outdoor Leisure, with each walk.

A lot is spoken about having the correct equipment for bad weather. There is no doubt that ideally you should wear good boots as well as weatherproof clothing. This is particularly important for the three walks that start from Rowarth, Edale and Bradwell! I realised last summer though that walking in hot weather causes problems as well. I often wear shorts and invariably when that happens I encounter beds of nettles and a surfeit of brambles. Be warned – you wear shorts at your peril. Some paths can become overgrown so bear this in mind in the height of summer.

Within each walk I have mentioned places available for refreshment. These may be pubs or tearooms and very good they are too. They are all located in the village from where the walk begins but you should not leave your car at the pub or tearoom except in the case of Edale and South Wingfield. Here, you can use their car parks provided you are going to eat there. Car parking locations are indicated in the text, but if they are full, or for some reason unusable, please ensure that you park your vehicle in such a way as not to be a nuisance to those who live close by. Finally, do please remember to remove muddy boots before you go for food and drink.

As before I wish to mention the support given to me by Balkees – her help and advice have been invaluable. To paraphrase Joni Mitchell – 'We'll walk green pastures by and by . . .'

Enjoy your walking.

Charles Wildgoose

ROWARTH

Length : 4½ miles

Getting there: From New Mills, which is just off the A6 north of Whaley Bridge take the Mellor road north. After 2 miles follow	the signs for Rowarth. **Parking:** There is a car park just as you enter the village.	**Map:** OS Outdoor Leisure 1 – Dark Peak (GR 011892).

Rowarth is off the beaten track at the end of a cul-de-sac. It nestles just inside the Peak Park – the boundary is just 200 yards from the car park. The village appears to have developed to provide homes for local millworkers and a quieter, more idyllic place is hard to imagine. Certainly the terrace of cottages known as Drinkwaters' Buildings built in 1812 is

quite delightful. The surrounding countryside is marvellous and it definitely merits the extra effort needed to get there. The Little Mill Inn is also worth visiting. It has had its share of tragedy – in the 1930s the then landlord was drowned when Rowarth Brook flooded and swept him away.

After passing through Rowarth the walk rises by a lovely stream to higher

---

FOOD and DRINK

There are unlikely to be many more splendid settings for a pub than that of the Little Mill Inn. To get there leave the car park the way you came and at the T-junction turn left down the road signed 'Little Mill'. The inn is open every day from 11 am except on Sundays when it opens at noon. There is plenty of choice for real ale fans with beers such as Banks's, Marston's Pedigree and Camerons Strongarm. There are specialities available especially in the evening when pheasant, duck and guinea fowl may be on the menu. There's even a children's playground. The inn dates from 1781 and at the side is an enormous waterwheel. Telephone: 01663 746305 or 743178.

Manchester takes the breath away. The return is just as enjoyable.

THE WALK

❶ Turn right out of the car park into Rowarth. Pass Drinkwaters's Buildings, dated 1812. Turn right in front of Anderton House built in 1797, and 80 yards after turn left beyond the Old Post Office. Walk forward on the path above the stream. Turn right at the gravel lane, cross a ford and shortly after turn left over a footbridge. Then turn right with the stream on your right. Ignore another footbridge on the right further upstream. At a track turn right over the stream. Some 180 yards later beside Grove House walk forward up

ground above. Eventually a spectacular view from Coombes Edge over Greater

Looking westward from Coombes Edge.

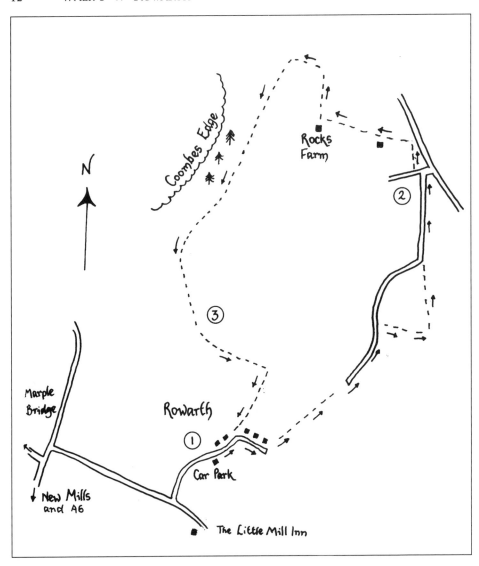

the lane for 350 yards past Ivy Cottage. Cown Edge Rocks come into view on your left. Turn right for 300 yards along a wide, walled track. Just before the gate across this squeeze through a stile on the left. Walk diagonally across the moorland for 400 yards in the direction of the point where the horizon disappears behind the heather ahead. The views behind are wide and impressive. Turn right on the quiet tarmac lane for 600 yards.

❷ At the T-junction climb the stile ahead. Walk forward beside the wall on the left. Continue forward where it bends left to the electricity pole at the top of the field and come out beside a road. Turn left for Higher Plainstead Farm and Rocks Farm. Walk along the drive passing the first farm, using the left-hand of the parallel drives. You may be able to say 'hello' to the friendly collie here. Stay on the drive to the second farm. Ignore a stile on the right as you draw near it and continue to the back of the house. Climb the steps on the right – leading up from the yard immediately behind the house – to a walled track. Just 40 yards later continue very slightly right to a large boulder 75 yards ahead. Bear right along a flattish grassy track rising steadily for 300 yards. Good views of Kinder Scout open out to the right. Bear left immediately beyond a second small quarry with a larger quarry on your right. This leads into a sunken lane. As you ascend gently an impressive view of Greater Manchester appears ahead including a number of high-rise buildings. Then descend gently to Coombes Edge – what a view! Turn left along a track parallel to the path over the fence. Stay just left of the plantation and join a grassy track with the trees 30 yards to your right. At the end of the plantation cross the stile and stay on the track for ⅓ mile. Cross a bridleway and keep on the clear path to another stile. Walk beside a fence on your right. Where it changes direction keep forward to the gateway ahead. Once through this do not follow the obvious path in front! Bear half right downhill towards a solitary house. Do not cross the stile in the fence above the property. Turn left and walk alongside the fence. Ignore a stile on your right as you do so. The path becomes

PLACES of INTEREST

After the walk why not hire a bike and ride along the **Sett Valley Trail** from Hayfield, 5 miles south-west of Rowarth. **Glossop Heritage Centre** to the north and **New Mills Heritage Centre** to the south are both worth a visit if you prefer something less strenuous!

a very shallow sunken green lane leading to another stile. Cross this and walk through a bumpy field. Keep straight forward as a most impressive view opens out. This provides a fascinating contrast between the hills of the Dark Peak on your left, the agricultural land ahead and Greater Manchester to the right.

❸ Descend to the end of the field where five paths meet. Pass through the gateway, taking the green track for 'Harthill'. The signpost here is erected in memory of Norman Ings – what a lovely way to remember someone who has gone before. The path you are following runs alongside the wall on the right. This becomes a sunken lane. After crossing a stile you reach a lane. Turn right on this for 300 yards back to Rowarth. Avoid all opportunities to turn left and right on your way back. In the village walk back to the car park.

EDALE

Length : 6¼ miles

Getting there: Follow the Edale road north from the A625 at Hope. Stay on this for 5 miles to reach Edale's village centre.	**Parking:** The pay and display car park in the village (or the Rambler Inn if you are a customer and ask first).	**Map:** OS Outdoor Leisure 1 – Dark Peak (GR 125853).

The village is a collection of hamlets – Nether Booth, Ollerbrook Booth, Grindsbrook Booth, Barber Booth and Upper Booth – all lying in the Edale Valley. In summer with purple heather to the north the scenery is most impressive. In winter it's just as attractive but when you get onto the hills hereabouts you have to know what you're doing. Edale is, of course, the start (or end) of the Pennine Way and our walk, although only a fraction of the length of the long distance path, involves a fair bit of uphill work, with views that make it all worthwhile.

After a climb to Mam Tor there is the chance to look down on the Hope Valley. A walk along Rushup Edge then gives splendid views into Edale and beyond over

FOOD and DRINK

The Rambler Inn is very popular, with food available in high season from noon until 9 pm. The low season serving times are usually from 12 noon until 2 pm and 6 pm until 8.30 pm. Gray's Best Bitter and 4.8 are served, among other beers. The food includes dishes such as steak and kidney pie, rump steak, farmer's pie and mild curry, with usually two or three specials in addition. Telephone: 01433 670268. An alternative is the Old Nag's Head, further up the village – they have the same owner. Telephone: 01433 670291.

Kinder. The descent of Chapel Gate leads to Barber Booth and a gentle return to Edale. Make sure you choose a good, clear day for this route – and it would be a good idea to try other walks in the book before this one if you are uncertain of your capabilities. There is a National Park Visitor Centre in the village.

THE WALK

❶ Leave the car park by the entrance and turn right on the main road. Follow it round carefully to the left towards Barber Booth. After 100 yards take the bridleway on the left for Castleton, 1¼ miles away. As you ascend, the ridge from Lose Hill on the left to Mam Tor on the right looms above. The bridleway passes Hardenclough Farm, a National Trust property. Look behind occasionally for the marvellous view towards the Kinder plateau. Ignore a number of paths on the right. Stay on the tarmac lane through a wooded area – it is basically a sunken lane at this point. At the next property, Greenlands, turn left over the stile and then immediately right. Greenlands is soon passed on your right. The stony track winds uphill

for ½ mile to the road. Turn left and walk through Mam Nick – the gap the road passes through. Beyond the brow of the road descend for 50 yards. Turn right at the National Trust sign for Rushup Edge. Follow the bridleway diagonally up the hillside to the top of the ridge. An impressive view of the valley opens out. Bear left along the ridge to its highest point. Away to the left is Eldon Hill Quarry whilst to the right is Kinder Scout and the first few miles of the Pennine Way.

❷ A stile brings you to the highest point of the walk at over 1,750 ft. The path then levels out before descending steadily and losing the view in the process. Look out for lizards hereabouts. After descending for over ½ mile you reach signpost 124 erected by the Peak District and Northern Footpath Preservation Society. Follow the arrow to the right for 'Edale via Barber Booth', ignoring the route straight ahead. The bridleway for Edale is sandy and fairly wide. Stay on this, ignoring small paths to either side. Some 275 yards after the signpost the bridleway bears right then left less than 100 yards later. Signpost 98 indicates the footpath for Upper Booth and Hayfield, but you stay on the bridleway for Barber Booth. Descend for ½ mile down Chapel Gate (as this track is known) – it is fairly steep. Head forward where the

PLACES of INTEREST

Just over the hill in **Castleton** are four caverns open to the public. They are Blue John, Peak, Speedwell and Treak Cliff Caverns. Not for the claustrophobic but a guided tour is well worth it.

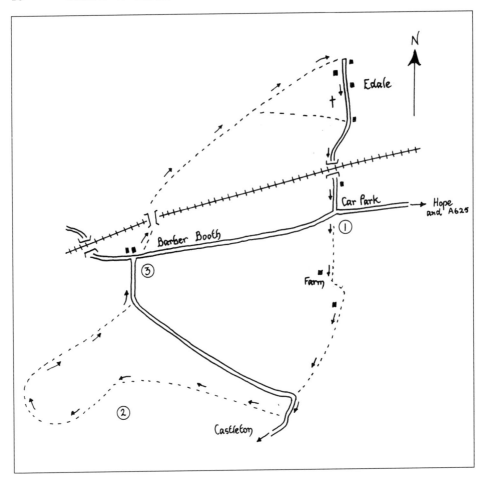

bridleway levels out. Ignoring a stile on the left, stay on the track as it winds its way to a lane. Descend this towards the houses of Barber Booth.

❸ Cross the bridge over the river Noe but don't follow the road round to the right. Take the left fork to the houses – the first one is Bakers Fold. Pass the Victorian postbox and bear right in front of the houses. Immediately beyond the brick house on the left walk up the farm track

which bends left to bridge 58 over the railway line. Just 25 yards after turn right through the kissing-gate and walk along the farm track. Look over your right shoulder to see where you've been – especially the distinctive 'V' of Mam Nick. Walk along the bottom side of the second field; then continue across the third field and along the bottom side of the fourth. In the next field, with Shaw Wood Farm at the top, bear slightly left to the stile opposite. Cross the bridge and the farm track

View of Upper Booth.

beyond and head for a stile 30 yards away. In the field beyond walk alongside the fence on your right for 10 yards. If you stay on this line you will reach Edale station and car park – you should bear quarter left off this path for the path leading to Grindsbrook Booth. Cross the field and continue over what appears to be a sunken lane (but isn't) to a stile. From here walk along the bottom of two fields and continue similarly into a third field to where the fence juts out. From here continue in the same direction across the field to a stile on the other side. Turn right down the track beyond this stile until you reach an open area where a number of tracks meet. Keep right to a squeezer stile beside a gate. Continue along the tarmac lane into the top end of the village. The Old Nag's Head lies uphill to your left – this is the official start of the Pennine Way. Turn right down the lane back to the starting point, passing the National Park Visitor Centre and the Rambler Inn as you do so.

BRADWELL

Length : 3¾ miles

Getting there: Either take the Bradwell road (the B6049) south from the A625 or north from the A623.	Parking: Use the village streets.	Map: OS Outdoor Leisure 1 – Dark Peak (GR 174809).

Bradwell's existence probably owes itself to the local quarries and leadmines. It is a typical Peak District village, full of interest with numerous little lanes and gennels to explore. There was obviously no grand design when it was built, all the older houses are different, and yet it all seems to fall together to create a fascinating whole. Opposite the church is the cottage where Samuel Fox, the inventor of the folding umbrella, was born.

After leaving the church the route follows the delightfully named Soft Water Lane before crossing the fields to the ancient Grey Ditch below Rebellion Knoll. Later there is an opportunity to visit the site of the Roman fort of Navio at Brough. A steep and steady climb leads to the high ground above Bradwell with far

---

FOOD and DRINK

The Valley Lodge is not far from the church and gives you an opportunity to enjoy good food with real ale (eight beers on offer at times, for example Barnsley or Coachman's Bitter). Food is available at weekends from noon to 2.30 and from 7 pm to 9 pm and sometimes in the evenings during the week. Besides the more traditional dishes – roast beef, gammon and steak pie – the Valley Lodge also provides something a bit different like Malaysian beef rendang or curry with pilau rice. This is apparently the only brick building in Bradwell – although you may be able to prove me wrong! Telephone: 01433 620427.

---

reaching views. Then although there is no sign of the actual cross itself you pass Robin Hood's Cross before descending from Bradwell Edge back to the village.

THE WALK

❶ The walk starts at St Barnabas's church. With your back to it turn right along the main street, and 100 yards later turn right into Soft Water Lane. Walk forward along this lane, avoiding the turn to Wortley Court. Beyond the British Legion building take the path to the right. Stay on this clear path across the fields with Rebellion Knoll above. The path generally stays at the same level until Grey Ditch – a raised bank across the path. It was apparently an Anglo-Saxon fortification. Keep forward in the same direction beyond this to reach a track at right angles to the path. Cross this and keep to the top side of Lee House ahead. Win Hill should be visible (weather permitting) 2 miles ahead, sitting like a pimple on the horizon.

❷ After passing Lee House bear very slightly left to a stile then forward to another beside a gate. This brings you onto a track leading to another stile by a gate. After crossing this walk forward, keeping to the right of a small tunnel which provides shelter for the sheep in all weathers. It is obvious that this runs for over 100 yards – the roof has caved in here and there. It appears to be a pair of parallel tunnels, or perhaps flues. At the end of the tunnels turn left downhill to the field bottom. Turn right inside the field along the track. Follow this round to the left and pass through a stile. Turn right in front of the houses to reach Town's St Ann's Well. This roadside water supply was presumably a spring rather than a well. About 200 yards away from this is the Roman fort. To reach it turn left to the main road and left again to a path on the opposite side of the road less than 100 yards away. Follow this path diagonally across the field to the remains of the fort.

❸ Our route from the old well turns right up Brough Lane. Where it bends sharp right after 200 yards keep straight ahead along the narrower lane. Cross a couple of stiles as the path rises steadily, then more steeply. The view of the valley behind becomes more impressive as you climb higher. Pass through a gateway where the path levels out and 50 yards later turn right up the drive to Elmore Hill Farm. To your left is Shatton Moor. At the top of the first field cross a stile (by an old bath!) to the right of the gateway. Walk directly towards the farm with the hedge on your left. At the top of this field pass through the gate into the farmyard. With a breeze block building on your right cross to the gate in the top right corner 20 yards away.

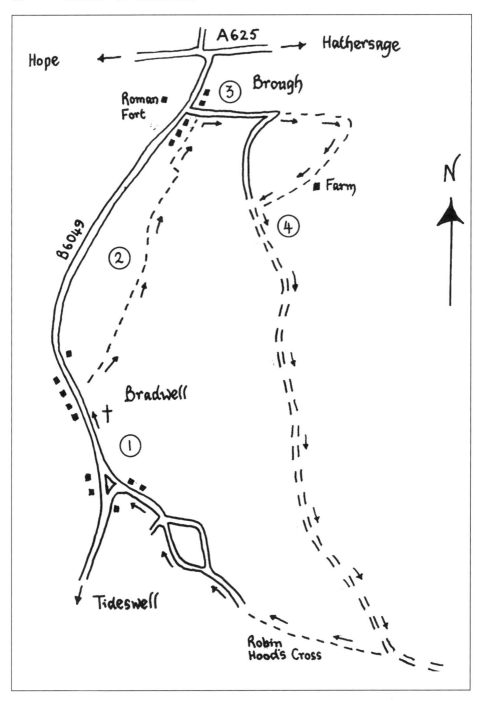

The cottage where Samuel Fox, the inventor of the folding umbrella, was born.

After passing through this bear left uphill, keeping a clump of trees on your left. Beyond these walk beside the wall. The view opens out with the Lose Hill to Mam Tor ridge visible, if there's no fog, and the Kinder Scout plateau beyond.

❹ At the rough track turn left uphill and follow it for the next mile. As you go look out for the continuation of Grey Ditch from the valley below. This is obviously an ancient highway you are now walking along, but how old? Pass the Derbyshire Wildlife Trust reserve of Overdale. Beyond the reserve, with a hill looming above you on the right, you reach a gateway across the track. Do not pass through this; turn right and negotiate the stile. Walk through two fields, with the wall on your left. In the vicinity of these two fields stood Robin Hood's Cross. This was massive apparently and the base of the cross is incorporated in the bottom of the wall hereabouts. At the end of the second field a wide view opens out. Walk down the path beside the wall to reach a bridleway dropping downhill from the right. Turn left down it. After passing through a bridlegate keep on the rough track downhill. Avoid a walled path forking right 100 yards after the gate. Your track bears left downhill, becoming a tarmac lane bringing you back into Bradwell. Keep left by a grass triangle to a small open area amongst the cottages – a little stream passes underground. Go forward past Ford Cottage on the right into Bessie Lane. Just beyond the Victorian postbox pass between the stone posts to descend the steps to the green beyond. Valley Lodge is now in sight or you can turn right to the church.

PLACES of INTEREST

Besides the caverns at Castleton (see previous walk) 12th-century **Peveril Castle** is one of the largest of its type hereabouts. It stands high above Castleton giving excellent views.

View of the Hope Valley.

TIDESWELL

Length : 6¾ miles

Getting there: Take the Tideswell road southwards from the A623 halfway between Baslow and Chapel-en-le-Frith.

Parking: You can park in the village streets.

Map: OS Outdoor Leisure 24 – White Peak (GR 153757).

Tideswell is a lovely place with a marvellous 14th-century church – the Cathedral of the Peak. It seems that no two buildings are the same in and around the main street and yet they all complement each other. An enjoyable hour or so can be spent exploring the village and its alleyways, indeed you could probably spend the best part of an hour in the church itself. At well dressing time the area is particularly busy. Well dressing is a custom almost unique to Derbyshire. It originates from a pagan thanksgiving for water. Do try and get along to one of the villages when the well dressings take place. The wells are dressed using flower petals, moss, lichens, maize – anything that is colourful and can be used. The well dressings in Tideswell

FOOD and DRINK

Poppies is a friendly small restaurant (with overnight accommodation) in Bank Square, just a stone's throw from the church. There is a wide choice of dishes, such as spaghetti bolognaise, savoury mince on toast, prawn salad, sandwiches and stir fry vegetables with meat, and several vegetarian options. For those who don't need to (or don't care to) watch their waistline cream teas are available. It is closed in January but for the rest of the winter it opens on Thursday morning and all day Friday, Saturday and Sunday. In summer it also opens on Mondays and Tuesdays. Telephone: 01298 871083.

usually take place on the last Saturday in June.

This walk provides an opportunity to walk through the glorious scenery of Tansley Dale, Cressbrookdale, Ravensdale, Water-cum-Jolly, Miller's Dale and Tideswell Dale – an excellent circuit with contrasting scenery.

THE WALK

❶ Walk along the main street past the church and the George Hotel on your left. Turn right into a lane signed 'Church Lane (The Cliffe)'. Climb this for a view of the church which is now below you. Follow the road round to the left and continue along this, away from Tideswell. To your right is some of the countryside you will soon walk through. Stay on the lane for about ½ mile. Opposite a narrow lane on the left follow a green lane downhill to the right. The flowers down here are lovely in spring and summer. The lane brings you to the bottom end of Litton. Turn right at the road. Immediately past Hornbeam Cottage take the path on the left. Follow this half

right across the hillside to the highest point in the field. Cross the stile and the lane beyond to another stile. Pass through this to the gap in front. Turn half left to a stile. Through the next few fields keep forward beside the wall on your left to the lane.

❷ Walk forward on the lane for about 150 yards. Where it bends left into Litton proceed along the track ahead – ignore the stile almost immediately on your right. About 250 yards from the lane cross the step-over stile on the right. Walk forward into the field. Bear slightly left at the corner of the wall 120 yards later. The high ground a mile ahead is Wardlow Hay Cop, over 1,200 ft above sea level. The path leads to a stile then descends into Tansley Dale, part of the Cressbrookdale Nature Reserve. Continue downhill. In springtime lovely orchids grow hereabouts. In the valley bottom cross the wall and turn right into Cressbrookdale. Part of this route is a permissive path – the public footpath rises uphill towards the village of Wardlow over the hill to the left – it later descends into the valley ahead of you. Stay on the valley bottom path. Eventually it enters woodland then you reach a wooden footbridge. This leads to the other side of

PLACES of INTEREST

Before you leave Tideswell do look round the church. If you want to venture further afield visit **Buxton** to the south-west. There are some magnificent buildings here including the Opera House and the Crescent. For younger members of the party visit the Micrarium where natural history comes under the microscope.

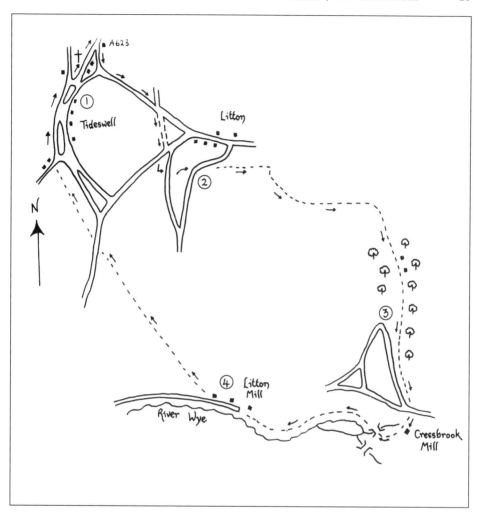

the wall. Stay on the obvious path down the valley. This brings you to Ravensdale Cottages. Behind these are the crags so popular with climbers. Continue along the tarmac lane away from the cottages.

❸ At the road turn left downhill to Cressbrook. Ignore all roads to the right. With a pond over the wall on your left turn right through the stone gateposts sur-mounted by a stone ball. This is signed 'Monsal Trail'. The path leads past the ruinous Cressbrook Mill with its belltower and clock. Keep on the right side of the yard behind the mill and cross a wooden footbridge on the right, ignoring another bridge to the left. Walk between the pond and the limestone rockface. Stay on this path through Water-cum-Jolly dale into Miller's Dale, walking upstream by the

Well dressing at Tideswell.

river Wye. Eventually you reach Litton Mill where the old factory is being converted into a complex for the disabled.

❹ Walk through the buildings to reach a row of houses on the right. Continue past them with the river on your left. Some 200 yards after the last house (and just before a small informal car park) branch right along the gravel path. Stay on this, rising gently through Tideswell Dale. Ignore a path to the right over a wooden footbridge after a few hundred yards. Cross the next footbridge 150 yards later and turn left. Continue up the valley to the car park (with toilets). Walk through this to a path continuing in the same direction beneath a line of beech trees. Follow this to the road. Turn right and walk along the pave-

ment for 200 yards – beside the sewage works! Just beyond this turn left through a stile and walk ahead for 20 yards, then bear right into the trees. The path rises to the far end of the field. Pass through a stile between two gates. Walk along the track until you reach the edge of Tideswell. At South View Farm cross the road to the lane in front and 50 yards later look out for the pinfold on the left – now a private garden. A pinfold is a small enclosure where, in days gone by, stray sheep or cattle were kept until the owner turned up to pay a fee to have the animal released. The man who looked after the pinfold was the pinder and this is where the surname Pinder originated. Stay on this lane past Gordon Cottage and proceed back to the main street.

SHELDON

Length : 6 or 5 miles

| **Getting there:** Take the road for Sheldon southwards from the A6 near Ashford-in-the-Water, then follow the signs to the village. | **Parking:** Park in the village street. | **Map:** OS Outdoor Leisure 24 – White Peak (GR 175688). |

This is a lovely upland village with one of the newest pubs in the county. It has one street with old houses and farms on both sides.

The walk is an upland one where the wind can be fairly fresh even on the hottest of days. 'Fresh' in Derbyshire can mean 'cool' but this is a circuit to enjoy and savour with its flowers in spring and summer, the limestone walls and stiles full of fossils, and the fascinating Magpie Mine just south of Sheldon. The route can be shortened to 5 miles by not visiting Monyash but this little village has a lot of interesting things to see.

FOOD and DRINK

The Cock and Pullet is easy to find in Sheldon. It opened in August 1995 and is named after the cockerels and pullets that used to run around in front of what is now the pub. It's a friendly place that walkers and locals have taken to. As it is open every day for drinking from 11 am until 11 pm (except Sundays when normal hours apply) you should never go thirsty. On sale are Bass, Stones and a guest beer now and again, plus Caffrey's. The food includes such dishes as steak and kidney pie, cumberland sausage and onion gravy (this is delicious!) and sirloin steak. There are also specials like pork chops in a cider, cinnamon and peach sauce. Telephone: 01629 814292.

THE WALK

❶ Walk westwards up the village street. Pass Top Farm and follow the road round to the left. As it gradually descends climb a step-over stile on the right. Walk to the far left corner of the first field. Cross the corner of the second field, then keeping in the same general direction, bear slightly left towards the wall jutting out in the third field. Continue in the same direction for the squeezer stile beyond. Keep in the same direction through the next four fields. The path then cuts across a field corner with the stiles 75 yards apart. In the next field head 35 yards to the right of an electricity pole ahead. The view of Deep Dale opens out on the right. Descend towards another electricity post at the bottom of the field. Before you do this look at the fossils in the top of the stile. Pass under the electricity lines to the stile at the bottom of the field.

❷ Turn left up the wide track. Cross the road and walk down the walled path opposite. Stay on this until you enter a field.

Proceed on the right side of the next few fields to enter a field with a wood on the right. Head in the same direction as before but after crossing the wall at the far side of this field turn left and walk beside it towards Monyash church ahead. Stay on this path to the edge of Monyash. (For the shorter route avoiding Monyash ignore the next paragraph and turn left down the lane at this point.)

❸ To visit Monyash – and it is worth it – turn right along the lane. At the T-junction turn left. About 150 yards later, immediately before Melbourne House on the right, there is a small building at the roadside. This is now a youth club but it was a Quaker Meeting House. The graveyard behind contains just a few simple headstones. Back on the road continue to the green in front of the Bulls Head. Turn left on the road for Bakewell. About 300 yards past the last house in Monyash turn left between a stone outbuilding and three or four largish boulders (just before the dip in the road) and cross a step-over stile. This leads into Bagshaw Dale – another dry Derbyshire dale. Walk up the path in the bottom of the dale to the lane where you entered Monyash. Turn right here.

PLACES of INTEREST

A few miles east is the lovely market town of **Bakewell** where you can buy a Bakewell pudding (they're not tarts!) or feed the ducks by the side of the river Wye. A visit to the Old House Museum gives a fascinating insight into the past including a look at the old Quaker family from Monyash, the Bowmans. The author is a descendant of theirs.

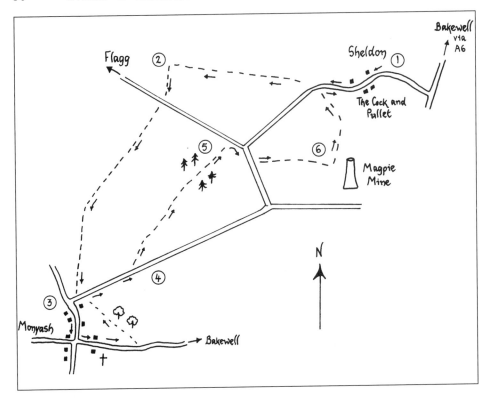

❹ About ⅓ mile along this lane there is a small wood on the other side of the field on the right. At this point pass through the stile on the left side of the road. Walk to the far right corner of the field. Pass through the gateway and bear right, walking parallel to the wall (on the right) to a stile across the field. Keep forward across the next two narrow fields. A trig point is just visible, 300 yards to the left. Bear slightly left to the far left corner of the next field. Pass through the squeezer stile. In the next two fields walk alongside the wall on your left but in the field after bear slightly away from the wall as the stile is 40 yards to the right of the corner. Cross the corner of the next field into the narrow wood stretching across in front of you.

❺ Leave the wood and walk along the right side of the two fields ahead to the road. Turn right and ignore the road to Sheldon. Some 200 yards beyond the T-junction the road levels out. Turn left over the stile by a gate. Walk forward, keeping to the left of a fence around a dew pond. Continue to the corner of the field. Pass through the gap and another one just a few yards ahead across the corner of a second field. From here head slightly to the left of the imposing chimney of Magpie Mine ahead. Cross the corner of the wall jutting out into the field – at present there is just

Magpie Mine.

a gap here. Head towards the mine, crossing another stile with a mineshaft near to it. In the grounds of this old leadmine head to a building made of black corrugated sheeting. Walk up the steps immediately before this. At the top of the steps is the winding wheel and the main shaft which is 729 ft deep.

❻ To return to Sheldon walk to the bottom of the round chimney. With this on your right and the main buildings behind walk to the far left corner of the field, passing an unusual low circular building 40 yards to the right. After crossing the stile in the corner of the field bear very slightly left in the general direction of Sheldon. A signpost in the far corner of this field indicates where the various paths lead you – take the one for Sheldon straight ahead. Pass into a small enclosure with a track stretching away to the right. Go through the squeezer stile just a few yards ahead. Walk up the right side of the field beyond, bearing right beside the wall to a step-over stile. From here walk diagonally across the field stretching away to your left. In the far corner enter the small wood, then on leaving this bear right to a tight squeezer stile beside a gate. This brings you back to the west end of Sheldon. Turn right to return to your car.

The Quaker gravestones at Monyash.

WALK 6

PILSLEY

Length : 6 miles

Getting there: Take the B6012 Baslow-Rowsley road and ½ mile north-west of Edensor turn onto the B6048 for Pilsley.

Parking: In the village.

Map: OS Outdoor Leisure 24 – White Peak (GR 241710).

Pilsley is a small village – so small it doesn't have a church although it does have a school and a pub. The excellent Chatsworth Farmshop and various craft-shops are nearby. Edensor, Beeley and Pilsley are the three main Chatsworth Estate villages, and although Pilsley may not be as interesting architecturally as Edensor it is still lovely. Most of the vil-lagers work for the Estate or once did so. During the summer Morris Dancers call here as well as horse-drawn carriages, the Lotus Car Club and three wheeled Morgans.

North of Pilsley the walk comes to the village of Baslow. After wandering through you turn south to reach Chatsworth Park and the marvellous setting of Chatsworth House itself – what an absolutely splendid

FOOD and DRINK

If you visit the Devonshire Arms on a Sunday get there early! It's popular and it's easy to see why. You have a choice of dishes such as roast prime cut of Angus beef, honeyglaze chicken fillet, Whitby scampi and salmon and cod bake. The real ale enthusiast will find Mansfield Bitter, John Smith's, Boddingtons and various guest beers. Lunch is available daily from noon until 2.30 pm. There is a carvery on Thursday and Friday from 7 pm until 9 pm – but please book for other evenings. Telephone: 01246 583258.

place. A gravel path leads to the model village of Edensor then up the road Celia Fiennes travelled centuries ago.

THE WALK

❶   With your back to the Devonshire Arms turn left down the road with the telephone box on your right. Walk 300 yards down the lane. Baslow, Curbar and Froggatt Edges are visible on the horizon. Opposite an old stone barn turn left over the wall (at present this is a poor stile). Walk on the left side of the wall towards a wood ahead. Just 20 yards before the end of the field turn right into a small enclosure and climb the two stiles a few yards apart. Descend the next field diagonally along the line of the telegraph poles. At the last pole bear left slightly to the footbridge partly hidden by the trees.

Chatsworth House.

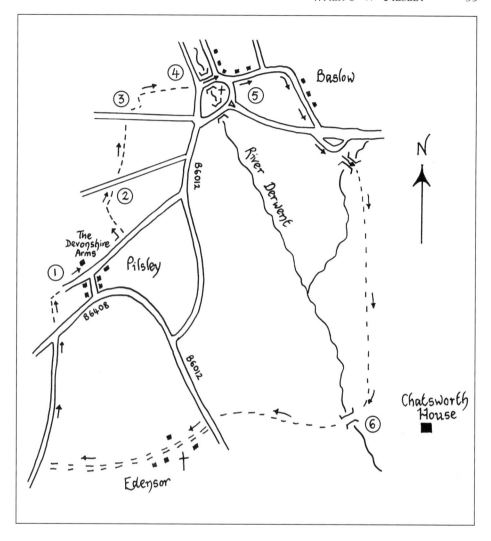

❷ Cross the bridge and road to the path opposite. Climb the first field, keeping just left of the telegraph pole. Walk to the far corner of this field. In the distance the Hunting Tower above Chatsworth is visible over your right shoulder. In the corner of the field are two gates. Pass into the field on the left and proceed beside the wall on the right. After 60 yards (where the wall turns right) bear slightly left across the field to the far right corner. (Many people walk round the field edge to the right at this point.)

❸ Turn right at the lane for 75 yards. Pass through a stile on the left and walk to the wall corner jutting out into the field ahead. Turn right when you reach it and

---

PLACES of INTEREST

If you've never visited it, then you have to go to **Chatsworth House**. You can also visit the farmyard and the exquisite gardens. If you like gardening then call at Chatsworth Garden Centre as you head south towards Beeley.

---

walk 100 yards with the wall on your left to the stile. Climb this and proceed through the next few fields with the wall on your left. A mile on your left, 'E' and 'R' can be picked out in the trees. The Chatsworth Estate planted these to commemorate the Queen's Silver Jubilee. At a water trough climb the stile beyond and walk between the houses to the road.

❹ Cross the road bridge ahead, noting the stone hut at the far side. Turn right in front of Tollbar Cottage. Immediately beyond turn right through a small gate to walk down to a seat. This affords an excellent view of the bridge. The church is worth exploring – it has two clocks. One has 'Victoria 1897' instead of numbers. In the porch is an interesting section of lead roofing and inside the church door is an ancient dog whip.

❺ Return to the road. Pass the churchyard on your right and walk to the mini-roundabout. Bear left up School Lane and 400 yards later bear right at the grass triangle into Eaton Hill. Stay on this and descend to the pelican crossing at Goose Green. Cross the green to the toilets on the far side. Turn left on the road in front of the toilets and walk forward to cross Bar Brook. Turn right beyond the

bridge on the track in front of a thatched cottage. Stay on this track to pass through a stile to reach Plantation Cottage on the left. Follow the path to the left, ignoring a path to the right, and 100 yards later pass through a tall kissing-gate into Chatsworth Park. Continue forward for a mile past White Lodge and then a cricket ground on your right. Later pass Queen Mary's Bower where Mary, Queen of Scots, was incarcerated.

❻ Just beyond Queen Mary's Bower pass through a small gate and turn right over the delightful bridge above the Derwent. On the far side take the gravel path to reach some large beech trees. It then bends right and descends to Edensor. Cross the road and pass through the gates into the village. Take the road to the right of the church. Follow this up through the village. Keep on the road as it continues to rise. It begins to deteriorate until it becomes a gravel track. Stay on the track for ⅔ mile beneath the overhanging trees. Immediately before a quiet lane look over the wall on your right for an old guidepost. When Celia Fiennes visited Derbyshire in the 17th century she wrote that 'You are forced to have Guides in all parts of Derbyshire' – hopefully, **you** will manage on your own! Turn right on the lane with wide views on your left. Descend to a T-junction after ¾ mile. Cross the road to a stile opposite and walk towards a low barn. This brings you to a grassy track. Walk on this for 300 yards to reach another track when you should turn right. After 100 yards you reach the edge of Pilsley. Keep forward to the Devonshire Arms.

BARLOW

Length : 4½ miles

Getting there: Follow the B6051 north-westwards from Chesterfield. Barlow is approximately 4 miles from the centre – as the crow flies!

Parking: On the main road near the church.

Map: OS Pathfinder 761 – Chesterfield (GR 345747).

A small village with an attractive church, Barlow lies between the lovely wooded valleys stretching towards the Peak District to the west and the industrialisation of Chesterfield to the east. An ancient pinfold stands 400 yards along the road running up by the Peacock.

The route follows a bridleway down to Barlow Brook. A ½ mile stroll beside this leads to an ancient stone bridge complete with mason's mark beneath. Then an easyish climb through woods beside the fishing ponds takes you further into the countryside. The last part of the walk passes the delightful Bole Hill House – a most charming property.

FOOD and DRINK

Hackney House Tearoom and Restaurant opens from 11 am until 4 pm from Tuesday to Sunday (inclusive). On Sundays it is best to book if you want a meal. All the food is made by the staff and there are starters, main courses such as cottage pie, fisherman's pie, lasagne al forno and vegetable lasagne, as well as salads, snacks and sandwiches. It's well worth a visit – and there are some delicious sweets. Hackney House is very easy to find being between the church and the Peacock. Telephone: 0114 2890248.

THE WALK

❶   Walk on the main road past the church on the left. This unfortunately appears to be locked when not in use. Keep forward on the lane where the main road bends left 250 yards later. Elm Tree Farm is on this corner. Just past Meadow Vale turn right down the tarmac lane. Stay on this for ½ mile. On the hillside ahead is the Chesterfield-Sheffield road cutting through the woodland. Follow the lane round to the left to some buildings. Just before them turn left through a stile by a gate onto a bridleway. (Do walk forward first to the bridge over Barlow Brook.) Back on the bridleway walk through the gate beside a brick building. Continue along the track by the brook for ½ mile to a lane. Turn right here, cross the brook and walk forward. Under this old bridge is a date stone presumably carved by the mason who built it.

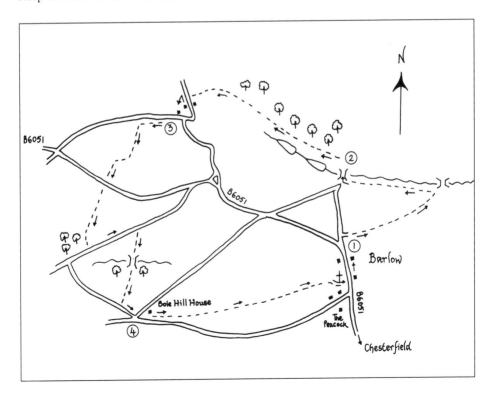

A friendly resident on the route.

❷ Keep forward past the entrance to the car park on the left – 10 yards from the bridge. A few yards later, just in the wood, fork left onto the path between two gateposts. Stay on this path and walk past a series of attractive ponds on the left. You may catch sight of some of the large goldfish in them. Just beyond the last pond a path cuts across the one you are on rising steeply to some steps to the right. Ignore this and keep forward beside a wall on your left. This eventually joins a track descending from the right – follow it down to the left. Join a lane 100 yards later, then turn right for 40 yards. Pass through a stile on your left and walk directly away from the lane. The path descends fairly steeply before bearing left downhill to some steps. Cross a stile on the left just beyond the steps, then descend to another stile and enter a garden. Keep forward to the right of a garage along a track which curves right to join another. Turn left here for 80 yards to a quiet lane.

PLACES of INTEREST

A couple of miles south of Barlow, **Linacre reservoirs** are set in woodland and provide an opportunity for a gentle stroll. Alternatively, visit the market town of **Chesterfield** to the south-west and wonder at the world famous Crooked Spire – visible from miles around.

❸ Turn right on the lane past Brind-woodgate Farm and 150 yards beyond the last building, where the lane bends right, take the path on your left. Walk down the left side of the field you enter and bear right to walk along the bottom of it to a squeezer stile. Turn left over Dunstan Brook to the lane ahead. At the lane walk diagonally left to a gate 20 yards away. There is a signpost here for Rumbling Street – a mile away. Take this path on the left side of the first four fields. Then walk up the right side of the fifth field – the wall in this field bears slightly left up to the road, Far Lane. Turn left down the road for ⅓ mile. Immediately beyond Far Lane Farm pass over a stile on the right into a field. Walk away from the stile – parallel to the wall on your right. Descend to a stile tucked away in the far right corner and enter a wood. Cross Crowhole Brook and follow the path uphill beyond the bridge. At the edge of the wood bear left beside it. Pass through the stile at the end of the wood. Walk straight ahead to the farm gate 250 yards away in the highest wall of the field. Pass through the stile by the gate and proceed to the lane. Turn left to the road junction 300 yards later and at the grass triangle take the middle of the three roads ahead.

❹ Continue up past a brick house 100 yards before the road bears right. Take care here, keeping on the left. As the road levels out turn left on the driveway of Bole Hill House. This is a really delightful property – built by the inhabitants of Barlo (sic) in 1677. Where the drive bends left pass through the gate on the right and walk beside the line of beech trees. This

brings you to another gate 70 yards later. (If there are crops in the fields ahead you may prefer to walk back to Barlow on the road you have just left. This will enable you to see some fine views to the south as well as taking you past the pinfold.) To walk through the fields continue forward in the first one beside the hedge. Where this begins to bear right keep forward to the stile in the wall, 20 yards left of the bottom right corner, although some walkers appear to walk round the right side of the field. Bear slightly left through the second field to a step-over stile. In the third field aim for the gateway ahead. In the fourth field walk forward to the right-hand of the two gateways. Then in the fifth field walk directly towards the church. This brings you to the sixth field in which you can walk down the right side. Cross a step-over stile and walk down the left side of the next field. This brings you to the churchyard over the wall on your left. The path bears right between walls to another stile. Keep forward from this to arrive back in Barlow.

BARLBOROUGH

Length : 7¼ miles

Getting there: From junction 30 on the M1 take the road for Worksop (the A619). At the second roundabout (by the De Rodes Arms) turn into the village. Follow the road past the church and the village cross.

Parking: In the vicinity of the post office or the village hall – or possibly in New Road.

Map: OS Pathfinder 762 – Worksop (South) and Staveley (GR 475773).

Some of Derbyshire's villages are indeed a revelation. In the centre of Barlborough is an impressive church (locked unfortunately), Barlborough House, Chandos Pole House and a village cross complete with plaque commemorating the community's fight to stay in Derbyshire – a most commendable (and understandable)

battle. The short extension at the end of the walk gives you a chance to see these on foot.

What an interesting area this is! After passing Barlborough Hall, there is the novelty of crossing the M1 by footbridge. A mile later you pass Park Hall, then Mount St Mary's College. The remains of

FOOD and DRINK

The De Rodes Arms, part of the Brewers Fayre Group, is attractive and worth a visit. A very wide range of food is offered. Battered haddock and fillet of salmon are just two of the fish dishes, then there are chicken dishes – balti and masala, for example – various hot platters, pasta and daily specials. There are also fresh salads and 'Light Bites'. Sweets are available too, of course. Food is served all day from 11 am (except Sunday when it's noon) until 10 pm. Four traditional ales are also on offer plus two guests weekly. Telephone: 01246 810345.

the Chesterfield Canal provide an unusual route into Renishaw before returning to Barlborough under the M1.

THE WALK

❶ Walk down Ward Lane with the village hall on your right. Pass the primary school and keep forward on the track. The view opens out with the M1 predominant – both visually and audibly! Ignore a track to the left but look out for the green dome of Mount St Mary's College. Pass through the woodland then alongside a high ivy-covered wall. A glimpse of Barlborough Hall is possible on the right. By the Hall keep forward (ignore a track forking left to a farmhouse). Look out for a footbridge over the M1 – you will cross this shortly.

❷ Some 600 yards beyond the Hall turn left through the hawthorns. Cross the M1 by the footbridge. Turn right beyond, then left beside the fence. Stay on the right side of the fence in this field and the next. Walk on the left side of the next fence by the trees. Turn right where the fence does – then left shortly after, walking away from

the trees. Approximately 350 yards later turn left again, still with the fence on your right. Cross a stile 100 yards on and walk down the left side of another fence. Ahead is Parkhall Farm. The dome of the college is now ½ mile away and the M1 is quieter. At the end of the field walk half left on the track to the farm. Ignore the first track to the right behind the farmhouse. Keep forward and take the second right between the farmhouse and Park Hall (with the high gable ends). Only a small part of the Hall is visible. Proceed along the drive towards the church at Spinkhill.

❸ At the road cross into Spinkhill. Some 75 yards later at the bus turning point turn sharp right. Follow the path between the wall and fence. At the road turn left for 50 yards. Take the first left through a narrow gateway into the grounds of the college. Walk forward for 20 yards with a house on your right. Then turn right. Turn left 25 yards later and proceed between the brick buildings. At the end of these continue downhill on a track with a high wall on your left. Follow this downhill and round to the left – ignore paths to right and left. Stay on the track as it curves right through the playing fields. At the far side you draw close to a hawthorn hedge on the left. Pass this on your left and follow the level track towards the large pylons ahead. Descend steadily under the power lines, then over

PLACES of INTEREST

Just one junction south of Barlborough on the M1 is **Hardwick Hall**. It is a breathtaking National Trust property built by Bess of Hardwick.

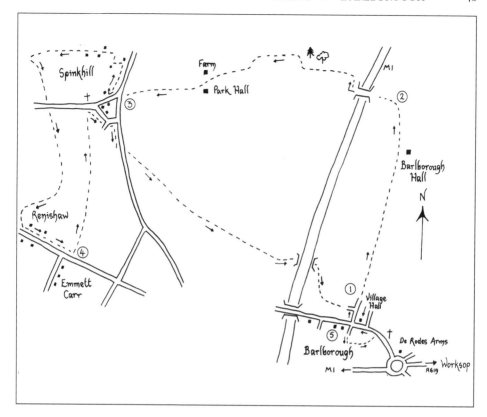

the disused railway line. Beyond the bridge turn left down the bridleway. After 100 yards fork left on a track onto the disused line. Cross directly over this onto the old canal and turn right. About 250 yards later cross the road and continue beside what remains of the canal for ½ mile. The path can be rather vague but if you continue forward – there are no sharp turns to left or right – you should be all right. Some of this section of path is quite attractive, some not quite so attractive beside the works! At Bridge 18 water is at last visible. You may wish to walk partway down the canal but our route leads onto the road above. Turn left along this.

❹ After ½ mile, 100 yards past Emmett Carr Lane descend the steps on the left. Walk up the path ahead for ½ mile into Spinkhill. Turn right here then right again into The Lane 50 yards before the Angel. Keep left at Park Farm Mews to the main road. Turn right down this for 150 yards and cross the stile on the left. Head half right across the field corner to another stile. In the second field stay in the same general direction to a gap 40 yards below the field corner to your left. From here stay in the same direction towards the highest tree ahead. At the bottom of the field keep left of Ingdale Farm in the trees – walk beside the fence behind it. Cross a brook

The attractive entrance to Chandos Pole House in Barlborough.

and enter a field. Proceed to a stile 100 yards ahead. Climb onto the old railway line and down the other side. Follow the path through the wood, eventually bearing left uphill to a field corner. Don't enter this field – bear right downhill along a path. Keep forward for 50 yards, ignoring a path on the right. Rise up a bank for 20 yards then head forward just right of a clump of trees. Cross a track to a stile ahead. Walk through the small trees and bear left up a bank to turn right along the obvious path around the field edge and pass under the M1. On the far side turn right into the first field. Descend to the bottom corner and climb the stile. Beyond this walk up the field, keeping 40 yards away from the house on the right. This path can become overgrown but eventually it brings you to a tarmac path – just to the right of the top left-hand corner. Turn left on the road beyond. Then turn right into Ward Lane and the start.

❺ An extension of 500 yards or so will give you a chance to look at some of the older buildings of Barlborough. To do this, continue straight over Ward Lane into New Road. About 200 yards later, just beyond Woodland Villas, turn left. This brings you out opposite the church. Turn right here for the De Rodes Arms or keep left, back to the start.

ROWSLEY

Length : 4½ miles

Getting there: Rowsley is on the A6 between Matlock and Bakewell.	Parking: In School Lane opposite the Peacock Hotel. There is more parking beside the playing fields further along the lane over the bridge.	Please do **not** park in the Caudwell's Mill car park. **Map:** OS Outdoor Leisure Map 24 – White Peak (GR 257657).

Rowsley sits astride the Wye and Derwent which join forces near the village. The first part of the route passes through allotment gardens and there is much to look forward to as the walk rises to Fallinge (also known as Fallange) with views of the Wye Valley and the A6 leading up to Bakewell.

This is one of the author's favourite walking areas. It is not particularly well walked which is surprising in view of the lovely paths through the countryside above Rowsley.

FOOD and DRINK

The Country Parlour at Caudwell Mill is a popular eating place. Try and sit near the window overlooking the millstream and the tree-topped mound of Peak Tor. The food is delicious and filling, and vegetarian and vegan dishes are always available in addition to some tasty cakes (the author recommends the chocolate fudge cake in particular). It opens during summer from 10 am until 6 pm and in winter from 10 am until 4 pm. Please note the Country Parlour closes during the week in January and February. Telephone 01629 733185.

THE WALK

❶ From School Lane walk back to the A6. Turn right over the Derwent. Cross the car park in front of the Grouse and Claret past the main entrance on your left. At the end of the buildings a stile takes you into a field. A signpost announces 'Public Footpath via Allotments to Beeley'. Cross to the stile ahead. Walk on the right side of the hedge and keep in the same direction for 300 yards. Just beyond the housing estate pass through a gap stile on the right and 25 yards later turn left for 300 yards – initially beside the allotments but then across rough ground into a wood. About 100 yards past a tumbled down stone building on the right, with the river to the left, fork right up to the road. Turn left for 400 yards. Ignore a stile on the right after 200 yards – continue to the Peak Park boundary stone. Turn right up the track through the second of two gates side by side just beyond this. Walk all the way up the track, ignoring a path across it. Continue into Smeltingmill Wood. This is a conifer plantation but not particularly well walked and quite charming.

❷ Bear left uphill for 100 yards or so, then turn sharp right – again uphill. This brings you to a high wall either side of the path. Pass between these. They were probably used as a ramp to tip spoil from Burntwood Quarry down the hill to the right. Follow the path as it heads forwards and bears left uphill to a gate at the wood's edge, then walk up the grassy track beside Smeltingmill Brook. This area is Fallinge.

❸ With a gate on your left turn right over the brook to the gateway to the immediate right of the farm buildings across the field. Pass through this and another gate immediately below a telegraph post 3 or 4 yards ahead. Walk on the right side of the small field beyond to a stile. Cross this and a brook immediately after. Keep alongside the wall ahead. Where it bears right walk slightly left to the stile in front of a large breeze block building. Climb this and follow the clear path along the right side of the building to the farmyard a few yards later. Walk forward a few yards then bear half left up the drive. Follow this as it bears right at the top of the field and levels out. Where it turns left proceed over a stile and walk beside a wall on the right. Some of the stones in this are set in the ground on their ends – presumably a quicker way of creating a boundary than the more traditional means. To the right you may be able to see Youlgreave church 5 miles away.

❹ Cross the stile into the last field before the road and walk to the far right corner. Climb the stile but take care – there is a ditch on the far side. Turn right then left a few yards later on the drive to the farm.

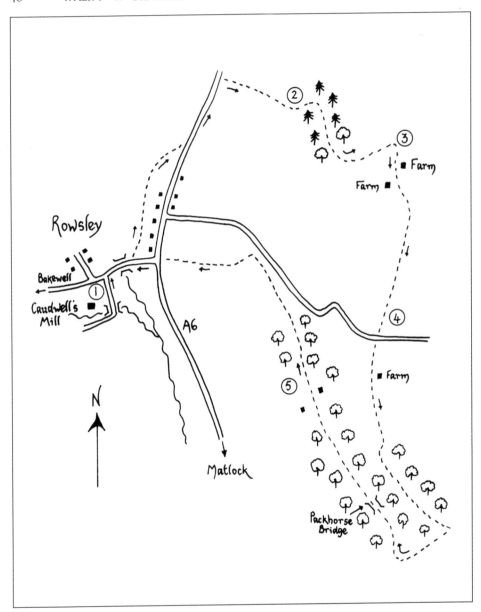

Look out for a sculpted face in the wall 120 yards from the road, just beyond a hawthorn bush. At the farm keep directly forward on a track with the farm over the wall on the left – do not enter the farmyard. Stay on the track to another gate beyond the buildings. Cross another field to a further gateway, then aim for a step-

An interesting stile near Fallinge!

PLACES of INTEREST

Caudwell's Mill is well worth a look. If you wish to make a day of it though head a couple of miles along the A6 towards Bakewell and visit **Haddon Hall**. Whilst you're there you can tot up the number of films and T.V. serials it has been featured in. *The Princess Bride* and *Jane Eyre* are just two.

over stile 20 yards right of the next gateway. Beyond, walk to the right of a building across the field. At this tumbled down building descend into the bottom corner of the field. Clamber over the very basic stile (little more than a wall). Turn right into the wood and 40 yards later pass through a small gate. After 5 yards turn left on the bridleway. Initially this rises through the trees of Northwood Carr before levelling out. Continue for 500 yards to a deepish gully on the right. Keep left of this then descend on the far side down a stony track – ignore the left fork rising away from the top of the gully. This track improves, becoming a tarmac lane between houses. Some 150 yards down the tarmac turn sharp right at a sign for Tinkersley and 150 yards later cross a packhorse bridge. After 50 yards fork left downhill through the trees. Stay on this track, ignoring others either side. Keep forward on the right side of a wall with an open field beyond. There are lovely views from here of Peak Tor – the small hill topped with trees in the middle distance. Pass through a stile into the field and stay on the grassy track into Tinkersley.

❺ Pass through a gate to a tarmac drive ahead. Turn right uphill and 80 yards later pass through the gateway of Tinkersley Farm. By a signpost for Rowsley Bar and Dale Road keep left of the first building and walk to a gate after 20 yards. Pass through a stile by this and walk beside the wall on the right. Cross the small field to a fence built in a gateway. This leads into Copy Wood. Proceed through the wood for 500 yards. It is unusual to meet any other walkers. At the end of the wood cross a stile onto a small golf course and turn right. Continue in the direction you've just come through the wood. This leads to a gate on the far side. Cross the stile by the gate and turn left downhill. Pass Toll Bar Cottage. At the entrance to Woodside a few yards later pass through a squeezer stile. Walk down the right side of the garden and continue downhill to the A6. Follow this back towards Bakewell and your car.

HOLYMOORSIDE

Length : 5¾ miles

Getting there: Holymoorside is 3 miles south-west of Chesterfield town centre. Take the A619 between Chesterfield and Baslow and follow signs for Holymoorside to the south.

Parking: In the streets near the Bulls Head.

Map: OS Pathfinder 761 – Chesterfield (GR 339693).

Holymoorside lies at the bottom of the hill leading up to Harewood Grange. Some people think it got its name from the monks who used to travel to the Grange across Holy Moor – perhaps. The old mill buildings where most of the villagers used to be employed have now gone. All that remains is the mill pond which is very popular with local fishermen. Holymoorside is an attractive village with beautiful surrounding scenery. The Bulls Head pub lies at the centre next to the village hall.

Beyond the mill pond the walk rises through lovely woodland to Stanedge golf course. Later the Great Pond of Stubbing

FOOD and DRINK

The Bulls Head is ideally positioned in the middle of Holymoorside and offers a wide menu. There are a number of low priced specials – such as haddock, vegetable lasagne, roast of the day, leek and potato bake and a 4 oz gammon – and many other dishes, sometimes including rabbit. Real ales are available. Telephone: 01246 588022.

is passed, then more woodland and field paths lead back to the village.

THE WALK

❶ From the Bulls Head take the road for Walton. Pass the United Reform Church. Turn right immediately past Mill Pond House. Follow the track into the field with the pond to the right. Beyond the pond head for the stile by the gate. Cross the footbridge and walk across the field then up the left side of the school. Turn left on the road for 150 yards. Where it bends right take the drive down to the left. Cross the river and fork right at a brick outbuilding. Pass through a small gate. Cross the track 10 yards away. Head to the stile leading into the trees 50 yards away. For ⅓ mile ascend through Gladwins Wood by a wall, then pass through a gateway and bear right to follow the path to the edge of Stanedge golf course. Turn left along the woodside. At the end of the trees walk beside a wall to a track with a pond

A view of Stubbing Court across the Great Pond.

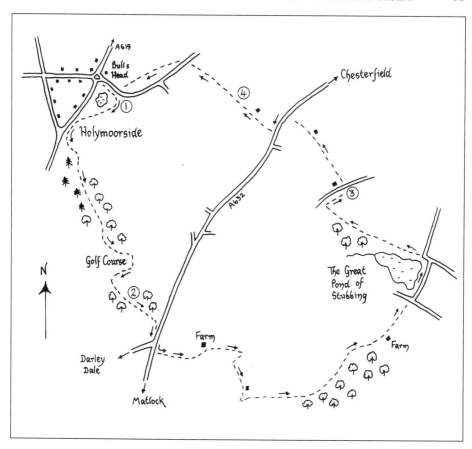

beyond. Turn right on the track to the buildings 100 yards ahead. Climb the stile and turn left uphill along the path to enter the trees 200 yards away – a noticeboard is there at present.

❷ In the trees follow the path bearing slightly left. This crosses a track 50 yards away and heads further into the wood. The path widens and rises steadily. Ignore a path to the right. Ahead the sound of cars will be more audible. Cross two more tracks when you reach them. At the road turn right, choosing the safest place to

cross, and 75 yards later go over a stile on the left. Walk down the left side of a small wood and the field beyond. At the track turn left towards the farm. About 70 yards later climb a stile on the right. Cross the field corner to a stile by a gate. Enter the farmyard and 40 yards after turn right over another stile. Walk 200 yards down the left side of the field to the trees. Cross a small bridge and proceed to the corner of a large wooden shed with a track beyond. Turn right on this, then left 50 yards later. Walk along the drive and turn right. Cross the wall at the far end. In the field beyond

---

PLACES of INTEREST

Chatsworth House, **Haddon Hall**, **Chesterfield**, **Matlock** and **Matlock Bath** are all within 15 or 20 minutes of Holymoorside. In addition Peak Rail runs steam trains between Matlock and Darley Dale Stations.

---

cross to the stile ahead – do not climb it – turn sharp left and head diagonally across the field. Near the far corner pass an oak tree on the left but do not enter the field behind it. Proceed through the gateway in front. Walk along the hedge on the left to another gateway. Cross the field to a gate directly opposite. Climb the stile and walk along the wall on the right for 250 yards. Pass through a gap by some holly trees. Bear half left to a hedge corner 100 yards away. Pass through a gap by a post and walk down the left side of a broken hedge. At the end of the field turn right to the far corner beyond the beech trees. Turn left and take the path between the walls. Follow the wall as it bends left to the farm. Proceed down the drive to the lane. To the left is Stubbing Court. At the Great Pond turn right then left over a single track road. Beyond the pond turn left on the lane. Where this bends right keep forward over the stile. With the pond below follow the path into the wood. Stay on the top-side of the wood – ignore tracks and paths to the right – and walk to the far end ⅓ mile away. There turn sharp right and almost immediately sharp left. Walk along the fence on the left, passing between two houses to the road.

❸ Turn right past Harper Hill House. After the last building turn left and walk down the left side of the field. Halfway down pass through a stile, continuing in the same direction but on the other side of the hedge. Cross a stream, turn left, then 75 yards later right. Proceed up the right side of a field. Climb a stile beyond the last building and walk left on the drive. Some 75 yards later where the drive bears left keep forward off the drive. Keep on the path (this can be overgrown) along a wall on the right to the road. Turn left for 200 yards past some houses. Beyond them go over a stile on the right and then a drive. Continue to the bottom left corner of the field. Pass through a gate and walk to a footbridge. Stay on the path to a stile behind the farm. Turn right to the top corner of the field past the farm on the right.

❹ Climb a stile and turn right. Walk along the right side of the next three fields – passing firstly through an obvious stile, then descending (and bearing slightly left) to pass through a gap in a hedge in a shallow valley. The next stile is tucked away right in the corner. The stile at the end of the third field is by a gate. From here descend along a broken hedge, bearing half left. After 80 yards by a gate on the right follow a broken line of trees towards a farm. Walk to a gate at the top side of the buildings. Cross the stile and turn right downhill. Keep left of the buildings and walk down the drive. At the lane cross to a stile. Walk along the bottom of the field beyond. Bear slightly right to a small gate. Cross a track and proceed along the bottom of another field. This leads to a track back to Holymoorside. At the lane turn right into the village.

TISSINGTON

Length : 4 miles

Getting there: Tissington is 3 miles north of Ashbourne just off the A515.	Parking: Use the car park on the Tissington Trail at the eastern end of the village.	Map: OS Outdoor Leisure 24 – White Peak (GR 178521).

A totally unspoilt village with no recent buildings, Tissington can be a honeypot for tourists but it is easy to see why. With its village pond and magnificent Hall it is obvious too why it is featured so often on Peak District postcards.

Although the village itself is busy this walk takes you away from the crowds – at least some of the time. After crossing the fields to Fenny Bentley there's a chance to visit the church with its unique Beresford tomb. Before that you will have passed Bentley Old Hall. A climb out of Fenny Bentley leads you to the Tissington Trail and a nature reserve where flowers abound in spring and summer. The trail used to be a light railway line running from Ashbourne to Buxton. It was closed in the

FOOD and DRINK

To reach the Bluebell Inn return to the A515 and turn left for 200 yards. It's a friendly and popular pub for anyone wanting good food, for example fillet of plaice, chicken kiev stuffed with garlic butter, chicken rogan josh curry and vegetarian meals. Draught Bass plus the local Black Bull Brewery's Dovedale Bitter are often available. Well worth a visit. Telephone: 01335 346463.

1960s but is now open for walkers and cyclists. Shortly after, a delightful path passes through Mill Pond Plantation back to Tissington.

THE WALK

❶ From the car park entrance turn right on the road. Pass the cottages dated 1840 and see the unusual use being made of some boots! The road passes over the Trail. Cross a cattle grid and turn half right to a farm gate 80 yards away. Head diagonally across the field beyond and pass through the squeezer in the far corner. Walk on the right side of the next field to a farm drive. Turn right on this, ignoring a left fork after 100 yards. Continue through a gateway towards Bassett Wood Farm. Stay on the drive as it bears right towards the farm. You will see the flat top of Thorpe Cloud – over 900 ft high – 1½ miles away.

❷ Climb the stile on the left as the drive enters the farmyard. Head to a stile by a gate ahead, then walk on the right side of the next two fields. As the ground falls away the view opens out with Fenny Bentley ahead. Climb the stile at the end of the field. Bear slightly right to a hedge corner 150 yards

ahead. Keep in the same direction for another 100 yards to the electricity posts. Turn right here to walk beside the hedge in front of the houses. Pass through the stile by a gate and follow the track to the road.

❸ On the left is Cherry Orchard Farm (formerly Bentley Old Hall). Cross the road carefully and turn right. Enter the churchyard by the lychgate. Walk to the top corner after looking in the church with the shrouded tomb of Thomas and Agnes Beresford. They lived at Bentley Old Hall and had 21 children – all of them shown around the bottom of the tomb.

❹ At the gate at the top of the churchyard turn left on the road. Beyond the houses turn right through the narrow metal gate. This is signposted 'Thorpe'. Pass through a similar gate at the top of the field. Keep straight ahead. When the hedge bears away to the right stay on the obvious path. As the path levels out the stile ahead becomes visible. Cross this and walk down the field with the hedge on your left. At the far end pass through a stile and head half right. This is a pleasant place to enjoy a little peace and quiet. The stile is 25 yards to the right of the stream.

PLACES of INTEREST

Ashbourne is a few miles south of Tissington on the A515. It is home to the unique game of Shrovetide Football played on Shrove Tuesday and Ash Wednesday every year when the 'Uppards' meet the 'Downards'. Feel free to join in – although at this point the author will disclaim any liability for any injury that you may suffer by getting involved! There is also some marvellous architecture in the town.

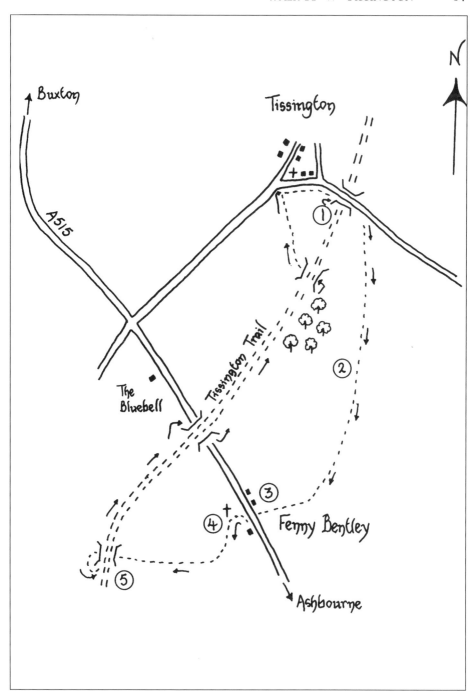

Tissington Hall.

Cross to the footbridge beyond and then a stile. Walk under the Trail and continue up the track for 100 yards, then turn very sharp left and walk past the Station House into Thorpe car park on the Trail.

❺ Turn left on the Trail and over the path you have just walked up. Continue for ¾ mile, passing through Fenny Bentley Cutting – a Wildlife Trust reserve. The road and the Trail start to converge. Just before the Trail passes over the road bear left off it to a farm gate 100 yards ahead. (If you prefer you can continue on the Trail for ¾ mile back to the start. This is easier but not so interesting.) If you leave the Trail cross the road carefully. Turn right under the

bridge. Just beyond on the left climb the stile by the gate. Turn left along the top side of the fields to a wood – the Trail is a few yards to the left as you walk this path. Enter Mill Pond Plantation. Keep on this path on the left side of the wood. Some 400 yards after entering the wood bear left under the Trail. Enter the field on the other side. From the stile walk diagonally right, heading just to the left of the buildings of Tissington. Cross three stiles that are quite close together. Beyond them walk along the left side of a stone wall leading away from you. At the end of this pass through the stile into a paddock. Cross diagonally to another stile. Turn right on the road to return to the start.

HOGNASTON

Length : 3¾ miles

Getting there: Hognaston is 4½ miles north-east of Ashbourne. Take the B5035 Ashbourne-Wirksworth road and follow the signs for Hognaston.	**Parking:** Park carefully near the church. Further parking is available 500 yards or so down the road beyond Brook House Farm.	**Maps:** OS Outdoor Leisure 24 – White Peak; OS Pathfinder 811 – Belper (GR 235505).

Hognaston church with its ancient tympanum – the carving over the entrance – is among several interesting buildings in this attractive village, which lies in an area of rolling countryside. The Red Lion is full of character inside and they have a ghost who is visible to some – but not others. If you spot a dishevelled, long-haired man in a trenchcoat with an ashen face you may be one of those who have seen it.

This short walk would have been very different a few years ago – Carsington Water has only recently been opened. After passing down the side of the church and climbing Enslet Lane to Uppertown

FOOD and DRINK

The Red Lion is a marvellous, friendly pub with excellent food and good beer (Old Speckled Hen, Pedigree and Marston's Bitter). The food is top quality with dishes such as fillet of steak in a 'Red Lion Sauce' and trio of lamb cutlets served with a Cassis and Madeira sauce. For a lighter meal you could choose, for example, a baguette filled with crispy bacon and warm Brie or smoked salmon and cream cheese. Food is served from noon until 2 pm (Tuesday–Friday) or until 2.30 pm at the weekend, and in the evenings from 6.30 pm until 9 pm (Tuesday–Saturday). This is becoming a very popular port of call so get there early. Telephone: 01335 370396.

the route changes character as you proceed along the side of the reservoir. The return along field paths completes an enjoyable ramble in a lovely area.

THE WALK

❶ Take the lane to the left of the church – between the church and Knowl House. Descend for 160 yards and fork right. Continue with terraced houses 30 yards to the left. Swing left after 60 yards over the ford and walk up a track, Enslet Lane. It becomes a grassy track which can be slightly overgrown. Ignore all stiles on the left as you rise. The track ends quite abruptly. Ignore a stile on the right as you leave it. Proceed through the narrow field ahead towards Uppertown.

Carsington Water Visitor Centre.

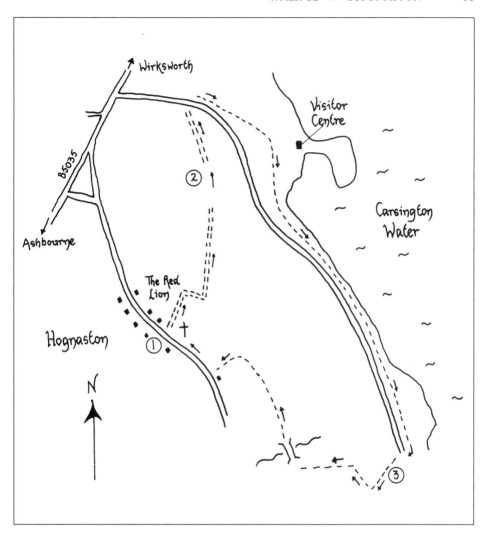

❷ In the top left corner of the field pass through the stile and walk onto the tarmac lane. Keep forward. Pass through the buildings of Uppertown Farm. Continue to the road. Turn right, walking towards the reservoir, and 70 yards later cross to the opposite side of the road and go down the track parallel to the road. This veers away from the road towards the Visitor Centre. At the tarmac road entrance bear left downhill towards the Centre. At the bottom of the slope turn right on the gravel track. This should have a waymark – 'CW3' – a reference to the third of five walks from Carsington Water devised by the Derbyshire Dales group of the Ramblers' Association. The leaflets are on sale at the Visitor Centre, where you will also find an exhibition, the Barrowdale Restaurant and information about water sports, bird hides, cycling and local wildlife – definitely worth a visit. In addition to the 'CW3' waymark there should be a sign for Millfields. Follow the track (and the Millfields signs). Cross the Sailing Club entrance. Walk past the boats with the road to the right. Beyond, keep forward on the banking which forms the dam wall – this section can be breezy! Over your right shoulder Hognaston should be visible. Continue to the far end of the banking past a tower in the water, then pass a viewing area on the left commemorating the opening of the reservoir in 1992. Continue parallel to the road towards Millfields car park – just before you reach it cross a step-over stile on the right – about 45 yards from the car park entrance. Cross the road to another stile opposite.

❸ Beyond the stile proceed between the fences. At the end turn right through a gap and aim just to the right of the village, towards a lone tree 100 yards ahead in the middle of the field. A waymark should show the direction to go but if it is missing keep in the direction you have just walked for a further 50 yards. This brings you to the remains of a hawthorn hedge. From

PLACES of INTEREST

You need look no further than **Carsington Water** to round off your visit to this area. In addition to cycle hire, water sports and bird watching, there is also an exhibition, shops and a restaurant to explore.

here walk half left to a gate in the field bottom. Cross the stile and follow the path to a gravel track. Turn left downhill and cross an access road. Some 50 yards later cross a footbridge over Scow Brook by a ford – a good spot for dragonflies. Rise up the track to a five-bar gate. After passing through resist the temptation to follow the track to the right – continue forward beside a fence on the left to a gap between fences. Once through continue to a similar gap. Cross a stile ahead and bear half left. Where the field begins to open out continue in the same direction, bearing slightly right, to pass through a gap in the hedge. Continue to a step-over stile in the top left-hand corner of the next field – 50 yards away. Cross this and walk across the next field to a stile with a small stone outbuilding uphill to the right. Cross to another stile and go over the track beyond. Bear half left to a stile in the field corner. Negotiate this, turn right and proceed to the road. Turn right to the church.

CROMFORD

Length : 3¾ miles

Getting there: Cromford is 3 miles south of Matlock on the A6. The market place in front of the Greyhound Hotel is just off the A6 on the Wirksworth road, the B5036.

Parking: In the market place. If full, park at the Cromford Wharf car park just before the church on the Lea Road – see map.

Map: OS Outdoor Leisure 24 – White Peak (GR 295569).

This is an interesting village. Just behind the Greyhound is Scarthin Pond and the walk passes this as well as Scarthin Books – a treasure trove of books, old and new. Then there's North Street, built by Sir Richard Arkwright for his millworkers. Arkwright was, of course, involved at the beginning of the Industrial Revolution. In the 18th century, his water-powered cotton mills ensured that things would never be the same again. Cromford has been home to other famous people including D. H. Lawrence and Alison Uttley who wrote the *Little Grey Rabbit* stories. Both once lived within a mile or so of Cromford market-place and Florence Nightingale didn't live much further away.

The route climbs uphill out of the

FOOD and DRINK

The Boat Inn is an attractive, traditional pub but they don't sell just traditional food. From time to time they have kangaroo and wild boar here – go on try something different! Or what about a medley of game in a mushroom and brandy sauce? Don't worry if you want something more down to earth – you can always choose breaded haddock, seafood lasagne or steak and leek pie. Definitely a very interesting menu. They also sell Old Speckled Hen as well as their own special brew – Boat Inn Bitter – alongside two or three other ales. The pub opens all day Saturday (11.30 am to 11 pm). For the rest of the week it's the more usual times. Telephone: 01629 823282.

marvellous views of the surrounding countryside. After a steady climb you will be pleased to walk down the High Peak Trail and finish with a stroll beside the Cromford Canal.

Please note: If you park at Cromford Wharf, start the walk at point 5.

THE WALK

❶ Stand·in the market place facing the Greyhound. Follow the lane leading to Scarthin to the right of it (a sign for the post office points along the lane). Walk on the narrow lane past the Boat Inn and Scarthin Pond. Continue and descend to the Via Gellia – the road leading from Cromford up to Grangemill. Cross this,

village before crossing the fields giving

Scarthin Pond.

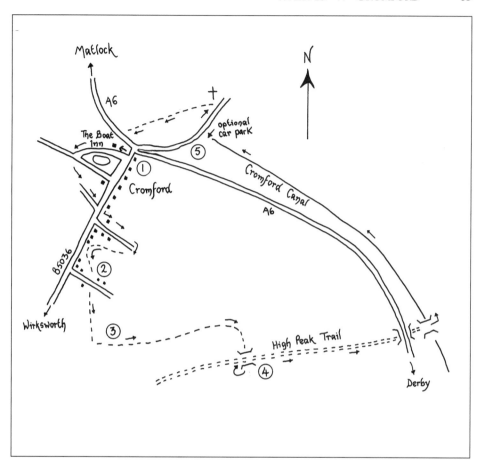

bearing slightly right. This brings you to a track leading steadily uphill. Just 25 yards later this narrows to a tarmac path. Proceed uphill through three squeezer stiles, then join a path running from left to right. Turn left along it to emerge at the top end of Alabaster Lane. Walk down this to a T-junction with Cromford Hill. The Bell Inn is visible to your right. Cross the road and walk towards it. The inn stands at the end of North Street, the street built by Sir Richard Arkwright for his millworkers. Walk along North Street to no 14 on the right at the far end. Turn right immediately beyond it to walk down the side of it. A few yards later turn right again. Follow the path along the back of the houses to reach a gravel track. Turn left here and follow it as it winds its way back to the main road. Turn left to Bedehouse Lane 60 yards later. Turn left into this lane, bearing slightly right as you do so, and 50 yards later turn right immediately after Sycamore Cottage. Follow the path between walls. Open fields appear on the left. Turn right beyond the bedehouses,

PLACES of INTEREST

A mile along the A6 is **Matlock Bath** with its Cable Car, Lead Mining Museum and Gulliver's Kingdom amongst other attractions. **Wirksworth** is just up the hill and here you can visit the National Stone Centre and the Heritage Centre.

then immediately left.

❷ The path becomes a tarmac lane, passing between some of the older properties in Cromford. About 150 yards beyond the bedehouses join another road. Walk slightly right across this and pass between houses 36 and 40. Ascend the drive until it becomes a narrow path, ignoring all turns to left and right. Some 200 yards from the road pass through a stile onto a track. Turn left and admire the view of High Tor and the redbrick chimney of Masson Mill – built by Arkwright. Pass Holly Cottage on the right then bear left beyond it. Proceed between two stone outbuildings. Beyond is a small water trough on the right. Also visible ahead is a squeezer stile leading into a small grassed area in front of two cottages. Cross to the squeezer on the far side. A glorious view opens out of High Tor, Willersley Castle and Riber Castle.

❸ Walk on a grassy track through two fields beyond. In the third field the track rises to the right of a rocky outcrop – Whiteley Rocks. It then continues beside a wall. With the outcrop on the left follow the track as it curves right to a stone gatepost at the end of the wall. From this proceed along a fairly indistinct path – this is just visible. Head towards the woodland at the far corner of the field. Cross a stile and proceed into the wood which is quite dark even on the brightest of days. The track beneath the tall trees descends before levelling out and joining another rising from the left. Turn right on this and pass under the High Peak Trail, then 50 yards after turn sharp right on a path leading onto the Trail. Turn right down the Trail over the track just used.

❹ Walk down the Incline for ½ mile and pass under the A6. Just before the road there is a catch pit on the right which was to catch runaway trains. Emerge on the other side at High Peak Junction. This is where the railway line and the Cromford Canal linked up. Cross the canal and turn left. Walk beside it for one mile. There is usually plenty of birdlife to see.

❺ Walk through the car park to the road beyond. Turn right to the church then left immediately before it. Follow the path, ignoring any others on the left. This takes you past limestone crags popular with local climbers. To your right is the Derwent and Willersley Castle. Continue to the main road, turn left and use the two pelican crossings to return to the market-place.

SOUTH WINGFIELD

Length : 3½ miles

Getting there: South Wingfield is 2½ miles west of Alfreton. Take the A615 Alfreton-Matlock road and follow the South Wingfield sign.	**Parking:** On the road to Tansley (Inns Lane), down Church Lane or, if you're going to visit the pub, in the small car park at the Yew Tree.	**Map:** OS Pathfinder 794 – Crich and Bullbridge (GR 375555).

The big draw in South Wingfield is Wingfield Manor House, recently made safe for people to walk round by English Heritage. A fee is payable but the Undercroft and the Great Barn alone make it worthwhile. Please note that you can only enter the Manor House when it's open – it is a private estate! The main village street is also attractive with some lovely old stone cottages.

This is a shortish walk that gives you time to savour the lovely scenery. Too many walkers walk too far and too fast – it's good to tarry awhile. After leaving the village the path passes under the railway line on a low (but short!) tunnel. Don't

FOOD and DRINK

The Yew Tree is a cosy, friendly and traditional village pub serving good food. There are usually three ales on offer – Pedigree and two guests – and dishes like ocean pie, vegetable lasagne, gammon steak and (if you're really hungry) a 32 oz rump steak are examples of the meals available. The Yew Tree has normal opening hours (lunchtime and evening) in the summer. Evenings only during the week in winter and spring, but on Saturdays it is open from noon until about 3 pm and on Sundays from noon to about 4.30 pm. Telephone: 01773 833763.

worry it's not dark. The walk runs parallel to the railway through a wonderful wood. The bridleway leading to the Manor House is delightful as well. As you walk along it try and imagine who might have ventured along here in centuries gone by.

THE WALK

❶ Assuming you park in Inns Lane walk to the centre of the village to Church Lane and turn left. (If you park at the pub turn right as you come out of the car park.) The road descends between high stone walls. Follow it round to the right and pass the Blue Bell. Away to your right Wingfield Manor House is clearly visible.

❷ Stay on the road over the river Amber at the bottom of the hill. Turn right on a path immediately over the bridge. Shortly after cross a footbridge. Walk on the left side of the river. Follow the path across the field to a kissing-gate. Pass through and continue forward beside a metal fence. After crossing this field go over the foot-bridge and pass through the tunnel under the railway line. Watch your head! Turn

right to walk parallel to the line, ignoring a stile on your left.

❸ Stay on the track beside the railway. When it bears left towards a house keep straight forward and pass through a stile by a metal gate. Shaw Wood is on the left with Wingfield Manor visible ½ mile away on your right. Pass through an unusual squeezer stile/gate by a farm gate. Continue straight forward, ignoring a more obvious path forking left. Cross a stile at the far end of this long field and proceed on the drive of an attractive property past a garage on the right. Where the drive bends right take the path on the left. Follow this diagonally across the field to a gap in the hedge. Cross the corner of the next field to another stile then to a foot-bridge in the trees. Cross this bridge and, keeping forward in the same direction, walk beside a hedge 40 yards in front. Keep the hedge on your right until you reach the end of it. Go forward here to a stile. Once through this cross the corner of the field and walk onto a lane.

❹ Turn right on the lane. Follow it for ⅓ mile. At another lane turn right under railway bridge no 53 some 100 yards later. This brings you into Wingfield Park. Take care on the lane here. Ignore a stile on your left on the far side of the bridge and

PLACES of INTEREST

It goes without saying that **Wingfield Manor House** should be visited. **Crich Tramway Museum** is only a couple of miles south-west. This is one of the finest transport museums of its type.

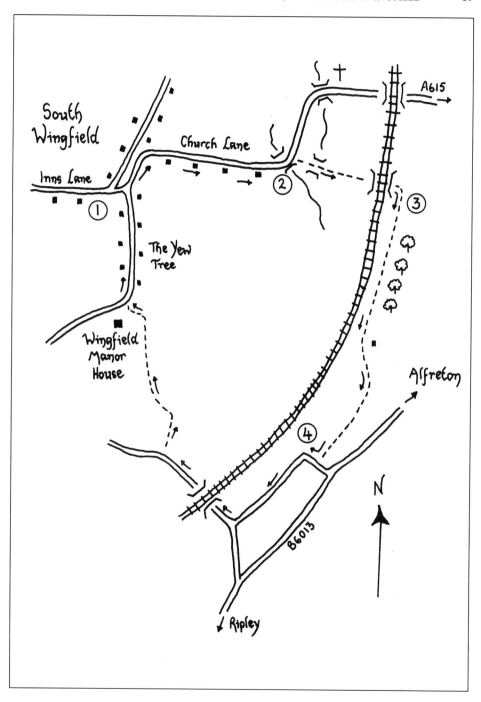

A footbridge over the river Amber.

250 yards later at a left-hand bend turn right on the drive which is also a bridle-way. At the entrance to Shrewsbury Cottage turn left into the trees. Cross a delightful ford as you do so. Stay on this bridleway for the best part of ½ mile. After passing between two woods keep forward – rising steadily – with the ruins of Wing-field Manor House above to the left. Where a track descends from left to right, the way back to the village lies downhill to the right. If you wish to have a closer look at the Manor House then turn left uphill. It is possible to gain access about 100 yards up the track – the entrance fee can be paid (at present) on the far side of the remains. The property is open from Wednesday to Sunday and Bank Holiday Mondays from April to October. Remember this is private property. Continue the walk by descending the bridleway to a level track. Turn left on this. Wingfield Hall appears on the right but do not turn towards it – keep forward beside a high wall on the right. This brings you to the main road into South Wingfield. Turn right along this back to the village.

The undercroft of Wingfield Manor House.

OSMASTON

Length : 6¼ or 4½ miles

Getting there: A mile south of Ashbourne turn off the A52 for Osmaston.	Parking: You can use the village hall car park on the right as you enter Osmaston.	Map: OS Pathfinder 811 – Belper (GR 200439).

Osmaston is one of the most attractive villages in the county – it must have the greatest proportion of redbrick thatched houses as well. When you add its village pond you can see this is quintessential England. If you're a photographer make sure you pack your camera because this walk offers a number of opportunities that you shouldn't miss. There is even an unusual wrought iron seat made of horse-

shoes by the pond. Most of the village is owned by the Osmaston Estate.

Initially the route follows the Bonnie Prince Charlie Walk down to the sawmill – a unique building in this part of the world. Some pleasant (and flat) lane walking leads to the village of Bradley. The church here is worth a visit and it is usually open, which is good to see. A good walk across farmland then brings you back

FOOD and DRINK

The Shoulder of Mutton is most unusual – it has a post office. (Don't worry – no jokes about the landlord stamping his individuality on the food.) There is a wide menu, including vegetarian curry or lasagne. If you prefer meat try the Brazilian beef or home-made Sicilian chicken. Bass, Pedigree and Jennings Dark Mild are the regular beers plus a guest which changes regularly. Telephone: 01335 342371.

THE WALK

❶ From the car park turn right. Pass the Shoulder of Mutton. Turn left in front of the pond and take the bridleway between the wooden gateposts – signed 'To Shirley'. This bridleway forms part of the Bonnie Prince Charlie Walk devised by the Ramblers' Association. It runs for 17 miles from Ashbourne to Derby (see also Walk 17). Follow the bridleway through a wood. Ignore a track to the left and later, as you descend, a crosstrack. In the valley is a small lake full of wildfowl with Osmaston Sawmill to the right, a most attractive building nestling in the trees. Climb up the bridleway beyond the sawmill – the

into Osmaston. An alternative option would be to miss out visiting Bradley and return to Osmaston after passing through Rough Wood, making a walk of 4½ miles.

Osmaston sawmill.

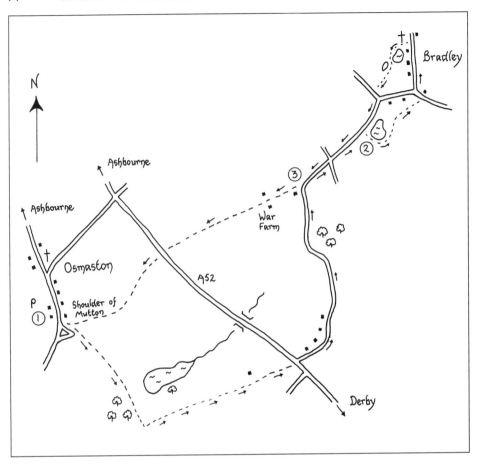

only steep climb on the walk. Where the bridleway levels out turn left on the track. This runs dead straight for ½ mile to Shirley Common Farm. At the farm proceed on the drive to the road, the A52. Take care crossing this and enter Rough Lane opposite. Walk on between the houses. Cross by the cattle grid into the open countryside and stay on the lane through Rough Wood. About ½ mile later turn right by a redbrick house on the left to the crossroads where you should cross straight over towards Bradley. (For shorter

walk turn left by the redbrick house and proceed to point 3.)

❷ Beyond a dip in the road rise gently for 100 yards. Pass through a kissing-gate by the gate for Knoll Lodge. Follow the path between fences with an occasional glimpse of a pond on the left. Where the path opens out continue beside the fence. At another gate in front of the house turn left and again walk between fences. Ignore a path to the right behind the house. Cross a stile into a field and walk to a farm gate in

PLACES of INTEREST

It goes without saying that a visit to **Ashbourne** is recommended. If this does not appeal then perhaps a look around the grandeur of **Kedleston Hall** near Derby will fit the bill. It is another National Trust property with which Derbyshire seems particularly blessed.

straight over.

front of a low brick building surmounted by a weather vane in the shape of a fox. Pass through the yard to the left of this building and emerge on the road. Walk up the middle of the three roads into Bradley. Pass the old schoolhouse. Continue to the church with Bradley Hall opposite. The path turns left in front of the church beside the churchyard – do try and visit the church if you have time. At the end of the churchyard pass through a stile and walk forward. Turn left at the end of Lady's Pond. Walk down the field with the pond on your left. At the end of the hedge cross the stile and continue with another pond on your right. Beyond this walk straight ahead to a stile at the end of the holly hedge in the corner of the field. Turn left on the lane. Shortly after turn right for Ednaston. Return on the road you used to walk into Bradley. At the crossroads keep

❸ Some 275 yards later keep forward by the redbrick house on the drive to War Farm 175 yards ahead. Walk directly through a number of gates in the farmyard to the field directly beyond. Go down the right side of the first field to an unusual bridge over the stream. Beyond this walk up the right side of the field ahead to a gate in the far right corner 750 yards away. In the wood to the left is Yeldersley Hall – though it is not visible. At the road walk right for 10 yards then cross over, taking care as you do so. Pass through a gap in the hedge. Keep to the left of a broken line of trees and walk directly away from the road. Aim for a small brick building in the field ahead. Continue directly past this to a footbridge in the valley. Head forward beyond it, rising through the field. (If there is no visible path from the bridge head just left of the largest tree ahead on the hill.) This brings you to a small fenced plantation. Cross the stile and walk to the far side – this path can get overgrown. Cross the stile on the opposite side. On the green lane beyond turn right uphill. Pass through the gate and return to Osmaston.

HEAGE

Length: 4¼ miles

Getting there: Follow the A610 to the east of Ambergate and turn off at the sign for Ridgeway and Nether Heage. In Nether Heage follow the sign for Heage and look out for a marvellous view of the windmill as you enter the village. At the White Hart keep forward, passing this on your left. The Heage Tavern follows soon after.

Parking: In the street near the Heage Tavern.

Maps: OS Pathfinder 794 – Crich and Bullbridge and 811 – Belper (GR 372505).

The main attraction in Heage is the windmill. This is owned by the County Council and has been open to the public in the past – hopefully it won't be long before it is open again. It has six sails and appears in good condition from the outside. The original Heage School is also passed on the walk. Incidentally they don't do things by halves in Heage. When three local men were convicted of murder in times gone by they hanged them together down the road in Derby – hence the local saying 'Thi' 'ang 'em in bunches in 'eage'.

The walk starts with an easy stroll

FOOD and DRINK

The village is off the tourist trail so many of the people using the Heage Tavern are from the area. If a 'local' is busy it's doing something right and that is certainly true of this one. The food is partly traditional with the steak and kidney with Yorkshire pudding and the seafood platter particularly good. The Indian dishes are very well spoken of too. Good beer – Bass, Worthington, Mansfield Bitter, Mansfield Dark Mild and a guest – is also on offer. Telephone: 01773 857235.

through the village and then goes down Bridle Lane from Upper Hartshay. Starvehimvalley marks the course of the disused Cromford Canal – see if you can spot its original line. The walk then passes through a short tunnel and continues along the canal before rising through fields to a stunning view of the windmill ahead. A lovely ramble in a rather unknown area.

THE WALK

❶ With the Tavern on your right walk on the road to the White Hart. Follow the road to the left to descend Tenter Lane. At the bottom of the hill proceed up Old Road past the Black Boy. Pass School House Hill to Lilac Cottage on the right. Turn left here on a track with playing fields on your right. Pass a playground and keep forward – ignore a path to the left. At the road turn right. Then 250 yards later, past a bus shelter, take the path for Upper Hartshay. Walk on the right side of a number of fields. Enter a field with a pylon 50 yards ahead. Immediately turn half left to a stile just right of a wooden electricity pole. Pass through this stile and with your back to it, head half right to another electricity pole. Pass through the

stile 25 yards before this. Keep in the same general direction towards the right side of a group of houses visible beyond the opposite side of the field. Climb the stile. Walk beside a hedge on the left. After walking between this and an oak tree bear slightly right through a gap onto a drive. Head up to the road. Turn left for 300 yards round a long left-hand bend.

❷ Cross to Bridle Lane on the right. Follow this roughish lane for ½ mile into the valley. After it levels out turn left immediately beyond a large green metal pipe at the roadside. Walk between the fence and some small gardens. At the end of the gardens is a signpost for Buckland Hollow. Follow the path into a second field. Head just to the right of a house ahead – this area is Starvehimvalley. Proceed to a fence and bear left beside it with the house now on your right.

❸ Pass under a fine old bridge and walk beside a pond on the left. At the end of this walk through what appears to be a long, narrow field, picking up a track as you go. This leads into some trees. Where the track forks, bear right slightly to a car park and a metal bridge. Pass under this into another car park behind the Excavator pub. Turn left here and walk parallel to the road on the right to a tunnel 100 yards ahead-part of

PLACES of INTEREST

The Midland Railway Centre at Butterley to the north-east promises a full day out for visitors. It is a working railway transport museum where beautifully preserved steam trains can be seen in all their glory.

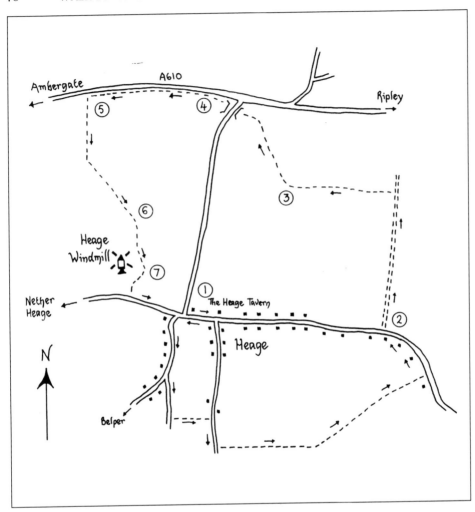

the disused section of the Cromford Canal.

❹ After a minute you should reappear in daylight! Proceed on the path past a small-holding. Look out for signs of the canal's stonework as you go. Ignore a stile by a gate on the left – proceed with the road over the wall on your right. The path is clear for the next ½ mile. Continue between hedges until you are walking by houses on the

right. Stay on the path between the allotments and houses of Ladygrove.

❺ At the entance to Lockwood Group premises descend the steps. Do not turn left. Follow the old road and cross the stone bridge ahead. Then proceed through a stile by a gate. Pass a redbrick house on the right to the path between walls ahead. Enter a field and walk up the right side. At

The windmill at Heage.

the end take the left of two stiles and walk diagonally across the field to a gateway. Here you will get a glimpse of the windmill. Pass through the stile by the gateway and turn right for 50 yards. Pass through another stile and head half left to a stile 100 yards away. Bear half right beyond this to a stile in a broken hedge. Walk to a green inspection cover. Pass through a stile in the fence beyond. Keep in the same direction to a stone post in the broken field boundary ahead, then beyond to a stile in the field boundary on the left. This stile is halfway up the hedgerow.

❻ Once through this turn right on a distinct path – the windmill is now out of sight. The path shortly joins a green track, which rises gently to a squeezer. Beyond this follow the path rising ahead. Away to the right is Nether Heage. To the left of a small clump of trees is a stile. Climb this for a great view of the windmill. From this point the OS map shows the footpath running across the field ahead – towards the unusual church tower. On the ground some people walk on the left side of the field for 100 yards before turning right for 200 yards to the stile.

❼ At the stile on the far side turn right in front of it. Walk along the hedge with the windmill to your right. Descend into the corner of the field and climb a stile onto the drive leading to the windmill. Turn left on the drive for 50 yards then left up Dungeley Hill past the Miners' Welfare building. Stay on this road past Heage School built in 1841. Pass the church and continue back to the start.

LONGFORD

Length : 2 or 4½ miles

<table>
<tr><td>Getting there: Take the A52 north-west from Derby. In Kirk Langley follow the signs for Longford. This will include 2½ miles on the old Roman road –</td><td>Long Lane. Turn left into Main Street, Longford.

Parking: Drive down Main Street. Bear left by the village</td><td>stores and park about 75 yards beyond the bridge.

Map: OS Pathfinder 832 – Derby and Etwall (GR 220374).</td></tr>
</table>

Longford is the sort of village you have to search for. No busy main road passes through it, which is to its advantage. Near the parking spot is the old mill – now a beautiful private house – and opposite is the former cheese factory, selling animal food these days. There are other attractive buildings, such as the pumphouse at the other end of Main Street, and more on the walk.

This short route can be easily extended to Shirley along the bridleway (For the extension head north for 1¾ miles on the bridleway and then follow the country lane beyond. Shirley is an attractive village with an interesting church. Return

FOOD and DRINK

To get to the Ostrich Inn return to the pumphouse at the end of Main Street and turn right. This is a popular and friendly pub, particularly nice to sit outside in good weather. The menu offers a wide range of dishes, including steak and kidney pie, curries, chicken and vegetable soup, fish, chips and peas, gammon steak, lasagne and scampi. There are also specials like chicken and mushrooms in black bean sauce. Marston's Pedigree, Ansells Mild and Marston's Head Brewer's Choice are some of the beers available. The pub opens daily. Telephone: 01335 330222.

the same way.) The village walk is very easy and clear to follow. After leaving the village it crosses Longford Brook and enters the Longford Hall estate. After passing through the farmyard do look round the church before continuing in front of the Hall and returning to the village centre.

THE WALK

❶ With the old cheese factory on your right walk on the lane. Opposite Cottage Farm on the right turn left through the squeezer. Walk between the fences beside the private drive on the right. About 100 yards from the road turn right across the drive. Keep forward, bearing slightly left through a paddock. At the end of a line of fir trees cross the stile. Walk forward through a gap in the fir trees ahead. This brings you 15 yards later onto a track. Turn left here. Some 75 yards later where the track bends right to a redbrick cottage keep forward into the undergrowth, bearing slightly right as you do so to a stile by a gate. Pass through this and walk diagonally across the rough field to the far corner.

This brings you to a stream and the Bonnie Prince Charlie Walk (see also Walk 15) devised by Derbyshire Area of the Ramblers' Association to mark the Ramblers' 60th Anniversary in 1995 and also the 250th Anniversary of Bonnie Prince Charlie's march from Ashbourne to Derby before he returned to Scotland. There is nothing to suggest he actually came this way, however. It is likely that his army (travelling the opposite way from you) would have passed through the countryside in a fairly wide swathe.

❷ Cross the bridge over Longford Brook and walk beside the hedge to the road. Go across to South Lodge and follow the bridleway along the driveway to the left of the Lodge. Some 300 yards later where the drive bears left pass through the bridlegate on the right. Keep in the same direction as you have just come and cross the field to another bridlegate. Beyond this keep forward along the right side of the field. After passing through a farmgate turn sharp left onto a rough track. (At this point you can continue along the bridleway in front for nearly 2 miles to the village of Shirley, returning the same way.) To complete the walk, follow the track to the farm buildings. After crossing the stream keep forward through the farmyard with the buildings on your right. This brings you to

PLACES of INTEREST

Sudbury Hall can be reached by travelling 6 or 7 miles south-west from Longford. Its stunning façade, interior and the Museum of Childhood make it a 'must see' attraction.

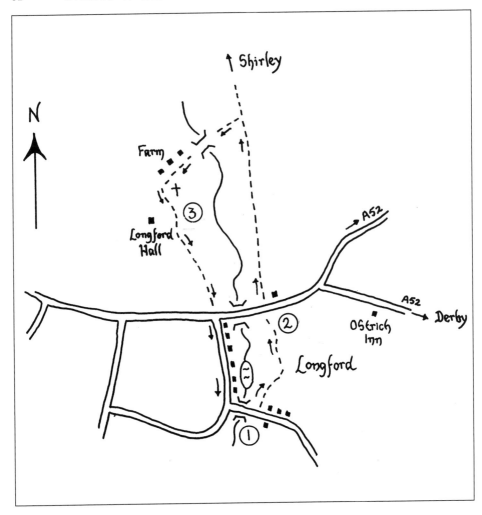

a courtyard (with its large working clock) on your right. Keep on to the edge of the churchyard. Turn right to walk between this and the last brick building. Enter the churchyard by the small gate and continue through it, passing the church itself on your left. If it is open it is well worth visiting.

❸ Leave the churchyard by the gravel path. Continue forward for a few yards along the drive to pass through the small gate by the cattle grid. Then keep alongside the metal fence and follow it round to the right, leaving the driveway as you do so. (If there is an electric fence here unhook it using the insulated handle – but reconnect it afterwards.) The path leads in front of Longford Hall on the right. Pass the large wrought iron gate to your right

The old mill at Longford, now a private house.

and pass under the electricity lines to the stream. Walk beside this to the footbridge. Cross this and turn left on the far side. Walk alongside the trees. With the ruins of a brick building on your left, bear slightly right towards the village 200 yards away. Pass through the gate onto the road and cross carefully. Walk down the village street. Where it bears left follow it round over the bridge. Quite often there are flocks of Canada geese hereabouts. Immediately over the bridge on your left is Longford Mill – a most attractive building. On the opposite side is the old cheese factory. A plaque on the latter reads 'This was the first cheese factory built in England. Opened on May 4th 1870 under the management of Cornelius Schermerhorn.' A nice way to finish a walk.

HOLBROOK

Length : 6 miles

Getting there: Holbrook is 2 miles south-east of Belper town centre. Take the A609 Belper-Ilkeston road. Turn off at Openwoodgate and 1½ miles	later go left into Chapel Street. Parking: In Chapel Street near the Wheel Inn.	Map: OS Pathfinder 811 – Belper (GR 363454).

Holbrook is a large village and although the Wheel Inn isn't in the centre you will pass through this near the end of the walk. The area around the Spotted Cow is particularly attractive and well worth exploring.

As with many places outside the Peak District most walkers don't know what they're missing in villages like Holbrook.

After leaving the built-up part the views are wide and attractive. The Hollybush pub with its old guidepost is a pub to return to and the route from Duffield Bank is interesting and varied. To sum up, it's fair to say this is another good route outside the Peak District – you certainly won't see the same number of walkers!

FOOD and DRINK

Much bigger on the inside than you might think, the friendly Wheel Inn is quite a revelation, and it's the sort of pub you will want to visit again. The real ale includes beers such as Timothy Taylor Landlord, Old Speckled Hen, the Mansfield range and Darley's. As regards food this is *entirely* home-made – even the bread. No chips are served but there is a wide choice including rice and vegetarian dishes, with more unusual items such as swordfish available. The Wheel opens 7 days a week. Telephone: 01332 880006.

THE WALK

❶ From the Wheel Inn walk downhill. At the T-junction turn left towards Kilburn. About 200 yards later at Ben's Farm

(where the road bends right) keep forward into the farmyard. Pass through a stile. Head forward beside the wall for 400 yards. Turn right through a stile immediately after Farm Cottage. Walk on the left side of two fields. Turn left through a stile at the end of the second field. Walk on the left side of a hedge; 30 yards later pass through a stile to continue on the other side to a farmyard. Go through a stile and proceed to the road.

❷ Cross the road and turn right. Fork left into Bargate Road. After 100 yards, beyond Chevin View, walk down the left side of the first two fields. The views improve into the Derwent Valley ahead.

The Derwent Valley.

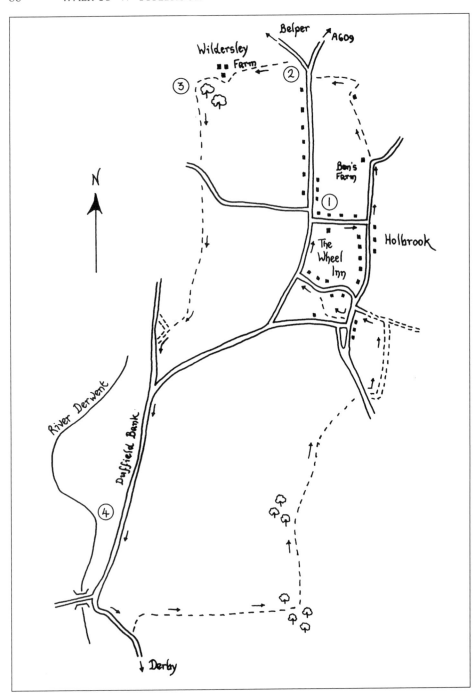

PLACES of INTEREST

Denby Pottery, with its visitor centre, lies just north-east of Holbrook. This well-known pottery was first made at the beginning of the 19th century.

Pass through a gateway into the third field. Walk on the right side of this and the fourth field. In the fifth field bear slightly left around the buildings of Wildersley Farm. At the end of the buildings turn right through a gate and a second one 20 yards ahead – this leads in the direction of the farmhouse. Walk along the track to the left of it but within a few yards descend to a stile on the left. Walk to the corner of the wood, then down the right side of it. Turn left on the path at the bottom of the trees.

❸ At the end of the wood proceed on the right side of two fields, then with a wood on your left to a lane. Cross this and follow the path forward. Where a field opens out ahead bear right to the lowest point. Pass through a stile and walk in the same direction as before. Go through the stone stile and walk beside the hedge on the right. Pass through a stile tucked behind a bramble bush. Turn left along the hedge to a stile 50 yards later. Walk along the top side of the field you enter then bear right to a stile by a gate in the bottom corner. Cross this into Dark Lane – the old Derby road. Descend to the Hollybush pub. Keep left of this past a stone marked 'Derby Coach Road 1739'. At the bottom of the hill turn left for 1 mile along the road. Ignore all turnings to the left.

❹ Descend towards Duffield church and the Bridge Inn. Turn left in front of the pub and rise uphill. Where the road bends right, turn sharp left at The Gatehouse. Proceed to the far end of the unmade road. Go down the side of house no 120. Follow the path behind as it rises steeply. At the top of the hill bear half right to a bridle-gate. Pass through this and proceed through the next four fields, keeping the hedge on your right – there is another path over the hedge – ignore it. Enter Eaton Park Wood. Keep forward until 50 yards later you reach a stile on the right. Turn left here to leave the wood 20 yards later. A path crosses the field bearing slightly left away from the wood. Follow this to a stone squeezer. Walk down the right side of the next field then along the right side of the wood beyond. At a squeezer on the far side of the wood walk slightly right to the cottage in the field beyond the one you are in. Cross the stile to the right of the cottage and go down the drive. Where the drive bears right pass through a squeezer on the left to cross the field corner into the wood. Walk through this into a field. Proceed through the middle of this towards an electricity post on the far side. On the road turn right then a few yards later left on the drive to Nether Farm. Follow this as it bears left. Pass Nether Cottage and Leaside then some farm buildings. Bear slightly right to subsequently join a track. Turn left up this into Holbrook. Turn left at the top past the Spotted Cow, then go right into Mellors Lane. Some 100 yards later turn right into Bradshaw Drive. Keep on the left side of this and continue across the open ground beyond. Proceed to the road. Turn left then right along Makeney Road. About 300 yards later take the second right back into Chapel Street.

WEST HALLAM

Length : 6 miles

Getting there: West Hallam is 2 miles west of Ilkeston. Take the A609 Belper-Ilkeston road and follow the sign for West Hallam (village).	Parking: In the vicinity of the war memorial.	Map: OS Pathfinder 812 – Nottingham (North) and Ilkeston (GR 432412).

The original village is fairly quiet being off the main A609. There is a very unusual and impressive war memorial and in the churchyard are two of the smallest gravestones you are ever likely to see. The Bottle Kiln Buttery Café is delightful and well worth visiting, and the Japanese Garden there is particularly lovely in the summertime. The Bottle Kiln also incorporates an Arts and Craft Centre.

This Erewash route is for those who like a gentle, steady walk – with no hills – and there's a great deal to be said for exploring this interesting district. You will have the chance to walk beside Mapperley Reservoir, then pass through Mapperley

FOOD and DRINK

To reach the splendid Bottle Kiln Buttery Café return to the A609. Turn left and the Bottle Kiln is immediately on your left. They concentrate on providing nourishing and healthy food, including some delicious sweets. Telephone: 0115 9329442.

itself with its stocks before returning to West Hallam through a quiet, secluded area.

THE WALK

❶ With the Punchbowl pub on the left follow the road round to the left past the war memorial on the right and 350 yards later turn into Scargill Road. Turn right on the path between houses 28 and 30. Follow this over a small culvert in an open area. Bear left beyond. Some 150 yards later cross a road and continue on the path opposite. Walk over another culvert towards house no 71. Turn right then almost immediately left up Chiltern Drive. At the top take the path to the right of house no 193.

❷ Turn left at the main road and 350 yards later turn right down the track beyond house no 49. Keep forward into the countryside – at last! Continue to the end of the first field. In the second keep just right of the hawthorns in the middle. Enter a third field and descend to the bottom corner. Cross the footbridge and head up the right side of the next field. Turn right along the disused railway line for 20 yards before descending the steps on the left, then head slightly right to the stile in Mapperley Park Wood opposite. Turn left immediately in front of the stile

and walk alongside the wood – do not enter the wood!. Climb the stile tucked round the corner at the end of it. Walk forward for 30 yards then turn left, keeping the hedge on your right as you rise very gently up a shallow valley. After a stile at the end of the first field go through a gap at the end of the second. Care is needed here! Instead of heading forward turn right through a gap into the bottom of a field opening out ahead of you. Walk up beside the hedge on the right. Some 200 yards along climb a stile tucked back into the hedge off the path on your right. Cross the narrow wood to another stile. Turn left in the field beyond to the gate. On the road turn left to Mapperley Park – a few houses. Where the road bears left turn right past the brick farm buildings. Walk down the two fields ahead, parallel to the right-hand hedge. In the distance the American Adventure Theme Park may be visible – or audible depending on wind direction. Cross the stile at the bottom of the second field into a large field beyond. Keep 30 yards to the left of a pair of oaks and cross the field to a stile. Turn right on the lane for 20 yards, then right on a path leading to a picnic area. Mapperley Reservoir, though not visible, is ahead to the left. Stay on the path into the trees – keeping

PLACES of INTEREST

Shipley Country Park is passed through on the walk. There is more to see though including the American Adventure Theme Park. This is popular with children who like frightening rides! **The Bottle Kiln** is well worth visiting too with its art gallery, craft and gift shops as well as a beautiful Japanese Garden.

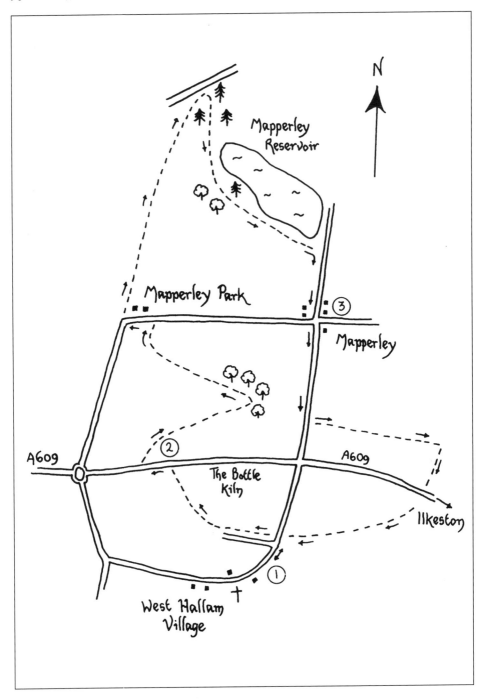

N

Mapperley
Reservoir

Mapperley Park

③ Mapperley

② The Bottle Kiln

A609

A609

Ilkeston

① West Hallam Village

A secluded area near Mapperley reservoir.

right at each fork until, with the reservoir on the left and open fields on the right, you reach a lane. Shipley Country Park is to your left. Our route turns right for Mapperley.

❸   Go straight over the crossroads in Mapperley. Pass the stocks commemorating the 700th anniversary of the grant of a Royal Charter for an annual fair and a weekly market. Descend towards the railway bridge at the bottom of the hill. About 200 yards past this turn left on the bridleroad for 'Ilkeston'. Pass the staddle stones at Brook Farm. Continue on the track through the woodland and the more

open ground for ½ mile. Ignore a lane descending to the left to some houses. Walk 30 yards beyond this and turn right up another lane, passing almost immediately over the remains of the railway line. Stay on this lane for 300 yards to the Newdigate Arms. Turn left for 120 yards, then cross the road to a track between house numbers 26 and 18 (Lewcote Cottage). Walk on this track for 375 yards, ignoring two tracks to the left to enter the field ahead. Walk down the right side of this and the one after. Cross the field behind the houses and climb the stile to come out on the road. Turn left back to the village.

MELBOURNE

Length: 4¼ miles

Getting there: From the A514 south of Derby follow the sign for Melbourne town centre. Go left at the Market Place and down into Church Street.	Parking: In Castle Street (turn left off Church Street) or in the vicinity of St Michael's church.	Maps: OS Pathfinders 852 – Burton upon Trent and 853 – Loughborough (North) and Castle Donington (GR 389251).

Melbourne is a large village, almost a town. The area around the church is particularly fascinating. In the space of a few yards you find the Norman church, St Michael's, Melbourne Hall and its gardens, a craft centre and Melbourne Pool. The church and the Hall gardens are open fairly regularly. The Hall itself is only open occasionally. Thomas Cook (THE Thomas Cook) was born here in the early 19th century and, of course, this Melbourne has ties with the bigger one in Australia – Melbourne, Australia, named after Lord Melbourne.

FOOD and DRINK

Melbourne Hall Tearooms is in what used to be the wash house and bakehouse of the Hall. These buildings were built in 1710 and some of the original brass is on display in the teashop, which serves morning coffee, snacks, light lunches and afternoon teas. There is a good range to choose from, with most of the food home baked. The teashop closes on Mondays (except bank holidays) and in January and February it only opens on Tuesday, Saturday and Sunday. Telephone: 01332 864224.

The walk is a very interesting one. The view of Breedon-on-the-Hill is a real surprise as you peek over into Leicestershire from Derbyshire. Then you walk along the Park Pale where King John is supposed to have hunted – this was a ditch with a paling on top that formed the boundary of the royal deer park. The return journey crosses fields before Melbourne Pool is visible with the church and Hall beyond.

THE WALK

❶ Stand in the open area before the church, then take the road for Wilson and Breedon. Pass Castle Mews and cross Carr Brook. Just 30 yards later go over to the path on the right. Pass through the kissing-gate and walk forward. After 15 yards bear slightly left through a line of trees running up the middle of the field. Pass through some more trees to a stile in the hedge. Just before this look right towards the Hall gardens. The Birdcage – a marvellous piece of wrought ironwork by Robert Bakewell – is just visible. Continue to the far left corner of the next field. Cross the cattle grid at the far side. Walk up the left side of the field towards two pylons. At the top cross a

track to a gap. A surprising view of Bree-don-on-the-Hill opens out.

❷ Head half left down the field to Wilson. Donington Park is in the distance to the left. At Green Lane turn right although you may like to turn left to walk around Wilson, a lovely village, before you do. In early autumn there are blackberries, sloes and hops along here. Stay on the lane past the golf club. This lane is the boundary between Derbyshire and Leicestershire. When the track swings right up to a farm bear left on a sandy track over a watercourse. Breedon church is ahead in the distance. Turn right to walk up a very shallow valley on a track. Eventually the bridleway runs alongside a hedge. Follow the track when it passes through the hedge. In this area there is a ditch beside the hedge. This is a section of the Park Pale – the boundary of an ancient deer park. The land outside was often higher than on the inside. Animals could get in but not out. After walking for 150 yards on the right-hand side of the hedge, pass through a gap to the left side. Some 200 yards later keep on in the same direction through another gap in a hedge across the bridleway continuing on the left side of the hedge you have been following.

❸ Shortly before reaching a mast bear right, then left to a quiet lane. Turn right

PLACES of INTEREST

After exploring the town and church of Melbourne, hopefully there will be time to look around **Melbourne Hall and Gardens** – note the most impressive wrought iron birdcage. If time allows do visit **Calke Abbey** to the south.

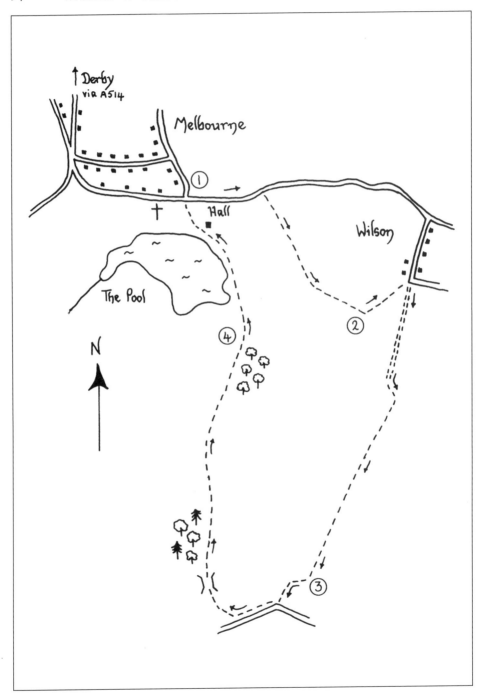

The tranquil route back to Melbourne.

down the lane. Just before a brick building on the left cross the stile on your right. Head towards the stile opposite. In the next field bear half right to the bottom right corner. Cross the stile then the stream beyond. Bear right down the valley, crossing another stile after 25 yards. Walk towards the near corner of the wood ahead. Do not walk beside the stream – bear slightly left away from it! Proceed with the wood on your left and cross two more stiles. Continue forward to join a track. This leads you (still in the same direction) through an avenue of trees. Beyond these, after passing through a gate, the track bears left to a farm – keep forward here down the right side of the field.

Cross the stile in the corner and turn right beyond along the hedgeside. Walk along the left side of Quarry Wood, keeping forward at the end of it.

❹ In the next field head straight forward. In the following field bear just left of the cottage. Pass through the kissing-gate. Turn left on the lane and, 30 yards after, right over the bridge. Before you cross this take the path on the left to admire the view of the church and Hall across the Pool. Return to cross the bridge and walk round the Pool past Pool Cottage. Turn right immediately after Melbourne Hall. This brings you to the church which is really worth looking at.